WHO MAKES A LEADER, NOT *WHAT*

ENRICH YOUR PROFESSIONAL PRACTICE & BECOME THE ACTIVE CHOICE ARCHITECT OF YOUR LIFE

Robert Andersson

Published by Robert Andersson,
Melbourne, Victoria, Australia

Copyright © Robert Andersson 2022

All rights reserved. Except as permitted under the *Copyright Act 1968*, (for example, a fair dealing for the purposes of study, research, criticism or review) no part of this book may be reproduced, stored in a retrieval system, or transmitted in any form or by any means without prior written permission from Robert Andersson. For further information, see www.rivenconsulting.com.au

Every effort has been made to trace and acknowledge copyright. However, should any infringement have occurred the publishers tender their apologies and invite copyright owners to contact them.

Cover design by Luke Harris, Working Type Studio
Layout by Lu Sexton
Edited by Lu Sexton
Cover photo by Finn Andersson
Printed in Australia by Ingram Spark

Andersson, Robert
Who Makes a Leader, Not *What*
ISBN print 978-0-6454424-0-3
ISBN ebook 978-0-6454424-1-0

Disclaimer
The material in this publication is of the nature of general comment only and does not represent professional advice. It is not intended to provide specific guidance for any particular circumstances and it should not be relied upon for any decision to take action or not to take action on any matter which it covers. Readers should obtain professional advice where appropriate, before making any such decision. To the maximum extent permitted by law, the author and publisher disclaim all responsibility and liability to any person, arising directly or indirectly from any person taking or not taking action based on the information in this book.

All stories in this book are based on transformations I have had the privilege to be part of. All names have been changed to protect the privacy of my clients.

About the author

Robert Andersson is a Swedish-born Viking who landed on Australian shores in 1994. He offers unique value and proven return on investment to any individual or organisation by pairing his research into unconscious bias with his highly developed entrepreneurial mindset and neuroscientific insights. Robert's lived experience informs his demonstrated authentic and human-centred leadership capabilities.

As an entrepreneur, Robert has been the founder of more than a dozen successful businesses across Australia and Europe. As a leader, Robert employs deep critical thinking, organisational sense-making, a 'not yet' mindset and systems thinking. Robert holds a Master of Change, Innovation and Leadership from Victoria University, Melbourne, Australia (2020) as well as an Undergraduate Certificate in Mental Health from Monash University, Melbourne, Australia (2021).

To my beautiful daughters, Rayna, Finn and Nyah, who remind me of what is important in life.

To my wife, Vanessa, who offers unconditional love and challenges me to grow every single day.

I respectfully acknowledge the Traditional Owners of the land in which I live and have written this book, the Bunurong/Boon Wurrung Peoples of the Kulin Nation.

I recognise the strength in leadership, courage and determination they have role-modelled in their efforts to maintain and preserve their cultures.

I pay my respect to the Elders past, present and emerging.

CONTENTS

INTRODUCTION	1

PART 1

1. WHY ACHIEVEMENT DOESN'T MEASURE UP	7
2. CONNECTING WITH YOUR INTERNAL LEADER	21

PART 2

3. SEEKING A DIFFERENT PERSPECTIVE	33
Exercise: Assess your perspective	38
Exercise: Information self-assessment	46
4. BUILDING HABITS THAT SERVE	53
Exercise: Ascending the five-step staircase	62
5. CHALLENGING UNCONSCIOUS BIAS	69
Exercise: Exploring your unconscious bias	72
Exercise: Spot the T-Rex	78
Exercise: Challenge your unconscious bias	86
6. TRANSFORMING YOUR INTERNAL LIBRARY	93
Exercise: Discover what's in your library	100
Exercise: Three steps to declutter your internal library	104

PART 3

7. THE TRANSFORMATION JOURNEY	115
WHERE TO FROM HERE?	135
EPILOGUE – THE EPIPHANY	137
CONNECT WITH ME	139

INTRODUCTION

Do you ever feel that you are drowning in a never-ending to-do list? Do you get a feeling of hopelessness when each task you tick off your list seems to be replaced by two new ones? Are you concerned that if you keep on working at this relentless pace you could end up burning out?

What if I told you that there is a way out of this abyss of doing-doing-doing, more-more-more?

What if I told you that you have the power to break free from this never-ending cycle of demands and become the *active choice architect of your own life*?

Would you be interested to know how?

By following the advice of this book, you will have the tools to make an informed choice about your future as a leader.

My role as a leadership mentor and coach is to guide and support leaders as they cultivate and enrich their professional practice and improve their wellbeing.

The process I use with them follows the leadership framework I developed over a number of years to transform myself. This transformation took me from an unfulfilled, burnt-out leader who was driven only by external achievements and had no connection to my inner self or wellbeing, to a leader who is connected to my authentic self, values my own wellbeing and that of my team, and whose internal motivations and values drive my external achievements.

For me, this shift from a purely external focus to a focus on internal and external leadership is the key to managing demands without risking burning out. Let me be clear and upfront about something here, I am not saying that external focus is bad and internal focus is good. It is perfectly okay to have a desire to be professionally successful in a particular industry or organisation. What I am suggesting is that the road to success looks very different depending on whether your values motivate your behaviours, or your behaviours drive your values. We will discuss the difference in a later chapter, but remember, balance is key.

Success does not have to come at the cost of all else.

This shift of focus changed my life, both personally and professionally. This is why I want to share it with you.

If you feel enslaved by the 'achieve-achieve-achieve' mantra that our society tells us is the only pathway to success, if you feel you are never going to get on top of your workload no matter how many hours you work, I want to show you another way.

Plenty of books describe this 'doing-more-achieve' merry-go-round model of leadership: the leadership status quo of the day. However, this book is about the road less travelled, it's about what I call internal leadership. I would love for you to come on this journey with me and activate your own choice. Together we can change the lens of what 'leadership' is, and as a consequence, the world will be a much more welcoming, safe and inclusive place.

My motivation for this book is to change the culture of workplaces and what is classified as leadership. I have three daughters and a wife and I am not going to leave the world looking the way it does. I want to purposefully drive the shift to enable women and vulnerable people to feel safe, be empowered and have the opportunity to blossom. A lot of my ideas align with my Swedish cultural heritage; Sweden is a place where women are empowered, supported by government policy and more equal than most. After all, 50% of Sweden's cabinet ministers are women and four out of five Nordic countries have a female prime minister.

My deep sense of the importance of valuing women stems from my mother. Not from the perspective of her being my mum, but for who she was in her professional career (she is now retired). She was a trailblazer for female leaders and her actions were motivated by her values. She was the first female mechanical engineer hired by her company, in the 1980s, and at most board meetings she 'dressed down' in a T-shirt with the slogan 'Without Women, Sweden Stops!'. Instead of seeing this as tokenistic and being the sacrificial pawn in a game of chess played by men, she embraced the opportunity and become the queen of the board! A lot of other women were hired by her organisation because of her trailblazing efforts. While writing this book, I discussed this with her and asked her if she would have done it differently a second time around. She reflected on the question and replied that today her T-shirt would have had a different message 'Without Women, the World Stops!'. My mother's strong views on what it means to be a woman in a leadership position have now global reach. I hope her message of being the 'queen' will help women break the mould on what it means to be a leader. It most certainly had a profound effect on me.

To support the validity of my leadership framework, I undertook extensive research while completing a Master of Change, Innovation and Leadership and an Undergraduate Certificate in Mental Health. Reading an extensive number of peer-reviewed papers and scrutinising tested models and frameworks has assisted me in writing this book. Academic research has added depth and breadth to my understanding and challenged my awareness of the many choices and drivers for human behaviours. This, coupled with my lived experience, has helped morph my leadership framework into what it is today.

And now it's time to share it with you so you can take back control and become the active choice architect of your life.

Are you ready?

PART 1

Let's start by looking at why achievement is not all it's cracked up to be and the difference between an achievement-driven leader and a values-motivated leader.

CHAPTER 1

WHY ACHIEVEMENT DOESN'T MEASURE UP

THE NORTH AND SOUTH OF LEADERSHIP

I was once drowning in work and focused on external achievements, you may be feeling the same way too. I thought I was chasing the dream, but really I was just chasing my tail. I'd bought the line that successful leadership is equated with achievement at the cost of all else. It's all externally focused. But even though I ticked all the achievement boxes – including reaching a childhood dream of becoming a millionaire – my so-called success wasn't making me happy. My externally focused goals were depleting my energy reserves and I was drowning, professionally and personally. When all of your energy is channelled towards external goals, the long-term costs to your health, vitality and happiness are often ignored. This unbalanced approach often leads to burnout.

In my quest to turn this around, I came to the conclusion that successful leadership is not *what* you do (external achievements), it's about *who* you are (internal motivations).

I define this as the north and south of leadership.

At the south end is the *externally* driven leader whose *actions and achievements alone tend to set the tone for their values.*

The actions and achievements at the south end of leadership stem from your external *WHAT* thinking; *WHAT* you are doing is the ultimate measuring stick. The south end of leadership cares more about a person's actions, achievements and the number of followers they have than it cares about *the person behind the doing*.

Through my reflections, I have come to conclude that the global system of measuring leaders is all too often driven by this all-consuming addiction to *external* growth via *external* achievement. I have also found that most organisations and governments are using external short-term, single bottom-line financial performance measures, rather than including the long-term environmental or social effects (triple-bottom-line). Similarly, the stock exchanges around the globe have created a culture where short-termism is treasured. This puts pressure on organisations and governments to perpetuate this short-term feedback loop, which in turn, translates into the expectations of leaders to do the same. Leaders in the short-termism model are often measured on their performance in the last quarterly report.

I was myself lost in a similar feedback loop at an early stage of my career, so I know first-hand how detrimental it is. Thinking about anything beyond getting past today, or this week can often feel like trying to overcome an insurmountable obstacle. Hours at work are often fatiguing and the demands are high. The little capacity you may have left beyond work is spent on the intricacies of life rather than self-care and recharging yourself. Personal wellbeing is not a priority; it may not even be part of your daily thought process. When you are busy fitting in and complying with the status quo, there is no capacity left for such intangibles. Personal wellbeing takes a back seat compared to achievements, all in the name of external growth, fast business and single bottom-line financial performance.

This is the way leaders are expected to operate, but is it sustainable? Working at the south end of leadership puts you at risk of becoming professionally, emotionally, spiritually and physically burnt out.

According to Asana's *Anatomy of Work Index 2021*, Australians had one of the world's highest burnout rates in 2020. A whopping 71% of employees experienced burnout at least once in the past year. Burnout has become so normal that the World Health Organization has weighed in and included it as an occupational phenomenon. During the 2020 COVID-19 pandemic especially, I saw my friends, family and colleagues face more burnout than ever through exhausting and endless online video conferences and meetings.

There's another way.

At the north end is the *internally* motivated leader whose *actions tend to be consequences of their values*. At the north end of leadership, the actions and achievements stem from your internal *WHO* thinking; *WHO* you are is uniquely valuable.

The thing that sets apart your external *WHAT*-driven leader from your internal *WHO*-motivated leader is your connection with your internal leader.

Your connection with your internal *WHO* motivates completely different actions and behaviours than *WHAT*-driven leadership.

When your goals are influenced by your *internal* leader your actions and achievements are consequences of your values.

Here are some examples of internally motivated leaders who are clearly driven by their values.

- Jacinda Ardern, New Zealand's prime minister, has led her country through a number of crises with compassion and empathy. Kindness is a hallmark of her leadership style.

- Vigdís Finnbogadóttir, president of Iceland from 1980 to 1996 (and the world's first democratically elected female president), worked tirelessly for women's rights. Her personal motto, 'Never let the women down', speaks for itself.

- Indra Nooyi, the first female CEO of PepsiCo (2006 to 2018) led by creating a vision, applying courageous innovations and releasing the power within each of her staff members.

Connecting with your internal leader may feel like an abstract concept. But take a moment to think about the last time you role-modelled leadership. Perhaps you led and managed an important project, supported a colleague at work or simply took the kids and their friends to the beach for surfing. What part of you do you think mattered to those who were under your care, your internal *WHO* part or your external *WHAT* part?

We all have an internal leader within us, but we need to have the relevant tools and insight to connect with it. This is what I want to show you. Connecting to your internal leader begins with an honest examination of yourself and your professional practice, and this book seeks to assist you to shine a light on the meaning and significance of this examination.

My leadership journey from a bleak, externally governed south-dweller to a self-regulating internally motivated north-sider is the basis of the leadership framework I use with my clients and what I am extending to you through this book. The messages in this book are not set in stone. They can be transformational and you must decide if you want to be an *active choice architect of your own life*, enrich your professional practice and improve your personal wellbeing.

> **An architect uses the power of their internal world to create and design structures around the world. By being an active choice architect, you are actively drawing from your internal *WHO* leader to create, design and influence your external world.**

Ultimately, leadership is first and foremost about introspection and connecting with the internal *WHO* part of yourself. Bringing *WHO* you are to *WHAT* you do elicits leadership; your *WHO* part is the quintessential elicitor of leadership.

A client of mine, Aiyla, led a small team of people and they always exceeded their quarterly targets. Despite all her leadership achievements, she was always overlooked for a promotion. Aiyla was a frustrated leader who felt trapped at work and this was causing her to burn up her energy reserves and feel rather flat at work. She realised that her current leadership approach was not getting her closer to her goal as a senior executive. Because of our conversations, Aiyla recognised that she allowed her external motivations to drive her behaviours as a leader. Her original mindset was to be given a promotion and *then* foster good working relationships with her colleagues and business partners – *the reward before the work*. We unpacked how being promoted to a senior executive would organically occur when Aiyla role-modelled her values through her interactions with others at work and focused on building strong foundations – *the work before the reward*. Sure, Aiyla always met her targets, but at what cost? She was always so focused on numbers that she forgot that business is about relationships, especially internal relationships. It was only when she connected with her *WHO* part and let her values motivate her behaviours as a leader that she became a senior executive within her organisation. With this balanced leadership approach, she successfully reached her goal while allowing her values to set the tone for her behaviours.

Now it's your choice to decide what kind of leader you will become!

THE RED PILL OR THE BLUE PILL

In the science fiction movie *The Matrix*, when Neo (played by Keanu Reeves) is being driven to see Morpheus, he's given a choice; to either get out of the car into a dark, rain-drenched alley or comply with having a live bug taken out of him. As Neo reaches for the handle to get out of the car, Trinity (played by Carrie-Anne Moss) reminds Neo that he has been down that road before and it leads back to the same place as always: a place of yearning and searching for the truth. Neo stays in the car and the trip continues to a house where he must open a door to finally meet Morpheus (played by

Laurence Fishburne) and find out what the matrix is.

This is where the movie gets interesting. Morpheus informs Neo that he can't be told what the matrix is, he must experience it for himself; just as Alice had to tumble down the rabbit hole into Wonderland. Once again, Neo is given a choice. Morpheus stretches out his hands, in one hand he holds a blue pill and in the other a red pill. If Neo takes the blue pill, he will wake up in his bed tomorrow morning and keep living life as he knows it. On the other hand, if he takes the red pill, he will find out how deep the rabbit hole goes. Morpheus makes it abundantly clear for Neo that all that he is offering is the truth, nothing more and nothing less. Neo briefly reflects and assesses the gravity of the situation before reaching for the red pill. At this moment, his curiosity is much stronger than logic, reason, the voice in his head or fear. The movie continues to follow Neo as he self-reflects, self-assesses and becomes self-aware of that which resides inside him: the power to stop the destruction of humanity and bring forth lasting change.

As a leader, do you currently choose the curiosity and change of the red pill or the comfort and familiarity of the blue pill?

The blue pill – are you lost in the matrix?

Are you ready to reflect on your style of leadership? If so, put on a helmet and be prepared for a bumpy road; waking up and listening is not always an easy undertaking!

Imagine a globe split horizontally into a red section north of the equator and a blue section south of the equator. These sections represent the red pill and blue pill takers. The blue pill represents leaders at the south end of the globe who are driven by external *WHAT* thinking. Their success is mostly measured by external achievement and *their actions set the tone for their values*. Consequently, their contributions are frequently aligned with self-interests.

Leaders in the blue section are regularly task-oriented. They often follow an empirical approach seen in the world of science and mathematics; one that is replicable, measurable and driven by data. They rarely question or reflect on their perspective, what they are doing, how they are doing it or why. Often, their actions and achievements require justification and anyone who challenges their perspective or actions is labelled a troublemaker or maverick.

As a young and immature leader, my addiction to the blue pills was equal only to my thirst for control. You can only imagine what kind of output you get when you mix two such toxic ingredients with a millionaire's mindset of MORE! I would 'lead' with equal measures of perfectionism and micromanaging just to see how far I could push people. Back then, I truly believed that leadership was all about *WHAT* you achieved in the external world.

There are different latitudes of blue-pill-popping, south-dwelling behaviour. For those closer to the equator, their choices and actions may simply comply with someone else's idea of what they should be doing: go to work and perform tasks that are neither enriching their professional practice nor improving their personal wellbeing. For people closer to the pole, which is all too common (and valued) in our society, their decisions and actions are influenced by careless self-importance. Many politicians fall into this category as their actions are driven by their eagerness to be re-elected rather than an eagerness to serve the people. The combination of the political system of democracy and the political culture devours any good intention someone might have. In the devil's den, you must behave like the devil in order to belong and move up the political ladder. For further reading on this topic, please see Niccolò Machiavelli's famous work *The Prince*. His motto 'the end justifies the means' has been adopted by many levels of business and government, as well as by individuals.

Is your professional practice locked into a system where the status quo controls your actions? How often do you feel that you can control or influence the status quo in a meaningful way? Is your personal wellbeing regularly overlooked in the name of fast business and external growth? If so, you may be unwittingly dwelling at the south end.

You may not relate to the extreme behaviours of the south-dwellers living at the pole, but if you feel you are stuck in a rabbit hole that leads back to the same place as yesterday, if you feel trapped by the status quo with no time, energy or ability for mindful self-reflection, self-awareness and self-regulation, then I have to break it to you: you've been taking the blue pill.

The red pill – are you ready to challenge the status quo?
In today's fiercely competitive landscape, it is hard to see beyond achievement-based leadership. You might not even be aware that you are choosing the blue pill daily; the matrix may have swallowed you completely. If you don't get this reference, I can only assume that you haven't seen *The Matrix*. Do yourself a favour, put down this book and put the movie on. I'll be waiting...

Back yet? Let me show you that there is another way!

The red pill represents leaders at the north end of the globe who are driven by internal *WHO* thinking. By choosing the red pill, you will shift from the external *WHAT*-driven leader to the internal *WHO*-motivated leader. Just like Neo, you will become aware of that which resides inside you by self-reflecting and self-assessing.

You may find that having one foot in the south and one foot in the north is a great way to start transitioning your leadership approach – one of each pill (talk about balance!). After all, purple is a suitable leadership colour. My client Aiyla definitely danced in a purple dress on the equator between north and south.

The essence of leadership is not a cookie-cutter model that you can replicate or measure. On the contrary, the art of leadership is internally purposeful, tremendously meaningful and deeply personal.

Over the years, hundreds of people have told me, 'Robert, I want to do what you did. I want to be like you.' My response is much like the above, leadership is not a cookie-cutter model; my journey as a leader is not the same as yours, and what worked for me may not necessarily work for you. Focusing on deepening *your* connection with *your* internal *WHO* leader is the key to starting your journey, not focusing on *my* connection with *my* internal *WHO* leader.

Your actions and achievements are spawned from a place of balance and connection with your internal leader. This contemplative introspection progresses you towards self-regulation and personal mastery. With enough practice, you will be able to let loose your internal leader in your private life as well as your work life.

Just as in *The Matrix*, you can't be told what *WHO*-motivated leadership is all about, you must experience it for yourself. To that end, this book is not a treasure map; there is no X marking the spot for *WHO*-motivated leadership. This book is meant as an invitation to begin the journey to embrace your *WHO*, connect to your internal leader and move north within your leadership. Before you know it, your internal leader will influence your organisation in meaningful and compassionate ways.

Are you ready to choose the red pill and begin your inner journey towards becoming the *active choice architect of your own life*, enriching your professional practice and improving personal wellbeing?

CHAPTER 2

CONNECTING WITH YOUR INTERNAL LEADER

IT'S NOT WHAT YOU SEE BUT WHO YOU SEE

Christopher Voss is a former FBI hostage negotiator and leader in his field. He argues that the primary question asked in most human interactions is: 'How are you going to help me?'. Once you understand this primary question it is easier to understand the BIG question: 'Do you see what I see?'. Implied in that is, 'If you don't see what I see, how are you going to help me?'

Voss says that in hostage negotiations, there is a five-to-ten-second window to answer the BIG question. Your response will determine the strength of the connection you will have with that person. If you demonstrate that you can see what they see, the connection will be *strong*; trust will begin to form and the negotiations can continue. If you can't see what the other person sees, the connection will be *weak* and the conversation will end.

In any human interaction, whether it's a conversation or a negotiation, it is not *what* you see but *who* you see! It's not about action, achievements or the length of your resume that matters.

What matters most is the feeling of assurity that you provide based on *who* you are, not *what* you have done in the past. Sure, in certain circumstances, past achievements and qualifications help, such as when applying for a job or a bank loan. However, it is ultimately the strength of the connection with your internal leader that is reflective of your *WHO*. The trust that forms and the feeling of assurity you can provide are two of the building blocks for mutual respect. You might not agree with the other person, but you are willing to actively and respectfully listen to their perspective and see the situation as they see it. Most importantly, you are willing to give up your need to be right.

SELF-REGULATION AND LETTING GO OF BEING RIGHT

In my south-dwelling days, I was so wedded to being right that I once deemed it appropriate to yell at a delivery guy just because he reminded me that the upcoming holiday period may mean that I needed to check my stock levels. From the perspective of my very tall, self-important pedestal, he was questioning my authority. Or worse, if he was right about my stock levels then I would be wrong! The cure for my egotism was learning to listen and letting go of my need for being right.

To let go of my need to be right, I needed to learn how to self-regulate my thinking, feelings, emotions and behaviours. This self-regulation required a degree of self-control. Sometimes when I was bombarded with work, my self-control buffer would become depleted to critically low levels. But with time I became **self-aware** enough to realise this. I learnt how to **self-assess** and **self-reflect** so that I could replenish my self-control buffer.

> **Through my personal experience and my work as a leadership mentor, I believe that becoming more self-aware, practising self-reflection and adopting a self-assessing state of mind are the keys to connecting to your internal leader.**

I have developed a leadership framework that I use to help leaders become more **self-aware, self-reflective** and **self-assessing**. Part 2 of this book uses this leadership framework to help you journey north and connect to your internal leader. But first, let me tell you how it came about.

MY STORY

Since I was six years old, my goal was to become a millionaire. With this external (and empty) goal, I set out into the world to achieve millionaire status. I created many business opportunities as an entrepreneur and eventually exceeded my initial goal. Thoughtful risk mitigation and professional curiosity have seen me engage in many different industries and disciplines including government, defence, mental health and community development, education and training, building and construction, service and hospitality and now being a published author. At its peak, this diversity kept me extremely busy and totally lost in the perspective of the external leader of doing more and as a consequence, *being* less. Eventually, I lost track of what was important to me and I spiralled down into a dark abyss.

Reflecting on this time in my life, I realise now how suppressed my emotions were. That millionaire dream was a desperate attempt to run from my troubled mind. Somehow, in my altered version of reality, money was going to provide me with the stability and safety that I yearned for and prove my worth and success to the world. It is now easy to understand how my parents' divorce and later on the death of my much-loved grandfather, Olof, devastated my world and what I perceived as safe. It is equally true that my thirst for external success was a substitute for the lack of worth and belonging I felt. My response as a six-year-old? I locked away all those hurtful emotions and channelled all my fears and anger into a millionaire's dream. If I couldn't feel safe within my family structure, the hunt for money and stability was going to keep me busy running from the darkness and the hurt. In time, millions of dollars were going to show the world how successful I was, which I believed was going to make me feel safe and belong. The house of cards that I created was built on repressed emotions and childhood trauma. It is only in retrospect that I now see how unhealthy my thinking was and how easy it was for me to buy into the doing-more-achieve mantra of leadership as a means to run from my trauma.

I eventually woke up and sought a different perspective. I then spent years crawling out of that dark abyss, challenging all my beliefs, habits, unconscious biases, perspectives and assumptions that imprisoned me in achievement-based leadership.

I didn't intentionally set out to take any particular steps in my journey to overcome my addiction to external achievement. It was more like the New Zealand hitchhiking adventure I'd taken some years earlier when each step in my journey was shaped by how far the next car could take me. Before I knew it, I was eating dinner at someone's house just because we connected via a hitchhiking thumb signal. Every time I was ready to move forward, the hitchhiking thumb went up to take me to the next destination in my journey.

This is how I developed my leadership framework, through my lived experience going from a south-dweller to a north-sider, with many bumps in the road! The leadership framework follows my metamorphosis from an eternally driven leader to an internally motivated leader.

I now use this leadership framework in my work as a leadership mentor, both in one-on-one mentoring and in group workshops. Applying this leadership framework to your professional practice will transform your perspectives, habits, unconscious bias and beliefs. It will enable you to become a more self-reflective, self-aware, self-assessing and internally motivated leader. When you are connected with your *WHO*, the ability to see and validate another person's perspective and their *WHO* comes to light.

THE LEADERSHIP FRAMEWORK

The leadership framework looks at four elements of your thinking and behaviour, your:

- perspective
- habits
- unconscious bias
- internal library.

Each of these elements influences your professional practice and has the power to either constrain you or set you free. We will be looking more closely at these in Part 2, with each skill having a chapter of its own.

Perspective

In the chapter on perspective you will be introduced to Peter Hare and Vanessa Longgame and their different perspectives of working *in* and *on* their respective businesses. For a perspective to form, we must have access to information and this information shapes how we lead. The key skill to seeking a different perspective is **self-assessment**. By entering a self-assessing state of mind, you can shift your mindset to effortlessly attract transformational moments that fuel you rather than drain you. Are you the tortoise or the hare? Let's find out.

Habits

Habits can either enrich us and help us live a fuller life or they can have us throw away opportunities and erode our valuable time. Our habits are driven by our assumptions, and these assumptions can support our external *WHAT* leader or our internal *WHO* leader. In the habits chapter you will discover whether you *hold your assumptions* or if *your assumptions hold you*. The key skill to identifying our assumptions and building new habits that serve us better is **self-reflection**. By reflecting on your habits, you can move from being an external south-dwelling leader to an internal north-side leader!

Unconscious bias

Our unconscious biases can warp our perspectives and imprison us with distorted thoughts and views of the world. Many of our unconscious biases are detrimental to ourselves, other individuals, communities and even entire countries! The key skill to challenging unconscious bias is **self-awareness**.

In the unconscious bias chapter you will meet your runaway T-Rex, which represents your unconscious biases running rampant in your mind. The first step in the subtle art of navigating unconscious bias and controlling your T-Rex is to unpack and come to terms with your own biases. By doing so, you can begin to understand why you think the way you do, and consequently learn why others think and believe what they do too.

Internal library

Our internal library holds the books of our beliefs, values, traditions and memories we draw from when navigating our environment. In the internal library chapter you will learn about the seed from which your internal library grows and the gremlin that ensures you hold on to this seed. The content of our internal library governs our professional practice. In this chapter, you will learn to declutter your internal library and shred the books that no longer serve you by *assessing*, *reflecting* and *becoming aware of* the content of the books. You will learn how to become the active choice architect of your own life and fire your gremlin!

Working through this leadership framework is not a linear process. As you develop the skills of self-assessment, self-reflection and self-awareness, you enter the cyclic process of self-regulation and personal mastery. All four elements of perspective, habits, unconscious bias and internal library feed into each other. As you gain insight into each one, you develop greater skills to reflect on or challenge another. This is a journey without a destination; learning is a life-long process. As you learn more, you free yourself from *you*.

At the end of these four chapters, which build on one another, I hope you feel comfortable using the leadership framework in your professional life as well as your personal life. Are you ready to get started?

PART 2

Now that we have established the value of shifting your focus from external *WHAT*-driven leadership at the south end to internal *WHO*-motivated leadership at the north end, it's time to look at how to do this.

I will guide you through taking inventory of your professional practice by assessing, reflecting and becoming aware of your perspective, habits, unconscious bias and internal library. This will help you understand the balance between *WHO* you are and *WHAT* you do, which in turn will help you connect more with your internal *WHO* leader. Be prepared to meet your runaway T-Rex and sneaky gremlin.

Each choice along this journey has its own consequence. As you connect more with your internal *WHO* it is easier to take responsibility and be accountable for these consequences. Applying this leadership framework to your professional practice will transform your internal library and ultimately enable you to channel your internal *WHO* leader.

CHAPTER 3
SEEKING A DIFFERENT PERSPECTIVE

Question: are you motivated by a sense of purpose or do you feel driven by a seemingly endless list of tasks?

DRIVEN BY TASKS VS. MOTIVATED BY PURPOSE

At the start of this book I asked you if you were 'drowning in doing'. If you answered yes, then chances are that you are working from an externally focused *WHAT* perspective.

I also suggested that there is another way. The key to that other way is your perspective. If your perspective is externally focused, you will always be struggling to keep all the plates spinning. Shifting your perspective from externally driven to internally motivated won't necessarily reduce the workload, but it will make it more **meaningful**. Instead of being driven by a seemingly endless list of tasks, you will be motivated by your purpose.

Rather than struggling to keep up, you will feel in control and ahead of the game.

THE TORTOISE AND THE HARE – A MODERN-DAY LEADERSHIP STORY

The hare

Peter Hare is a fast moving and efficient business owner. He lives by the action-man mantra and is agile in his approach. Every day starts with him checking his business emails and social media accounts. Based on this, he prepares a list of priorities for the day and responds accordingly. As the day progresses, he receives more and more emails and phone calls that require him to organise and follow up on orders and business service requests.

Three years into this business venture, the business is booming and Peter is constantly working in an operational capacity. At the end of each day, when the phone stops ringing and there are no more urgent emails to respond to, he needs to stay on top of stock levels, bookkeeping, accounts receivable and payable and check in with his staff. Peter feels in control when he spends his day working *in* his business. However, he also feels stuck as his vision board receives no attention and he is too tired to take any decisive action to facilitate growth. When he started his business, he had grand plans for the future, but now it is more about surviving the onslaught of business each day. Peter's biggest worry is that business will slow down and he will have to close up shop.

Peter is a task-driven external leader. His time perspective is short-term, ranging from daily to perhaps monthly goals and objectives. It's all about the action and the doing. As a consequence of his reactive approach to business, he spends his time making sure his staff is doing what they are supposed to and his main focus and priority is the day-to-day operations.

Leaders who work this way are often fighting uphill battles against external forces that are outside their circle of control. The job of managing the organisation is performed and it may stay alive for a while, but is it sustainable in the long term?

The tortoise
Vanessa Longgame put in endless hours and sacrificed a lot of time to build her business from scratch. She spends most mornings checking out trends and understanding consumer choices and behaviours towards certain products on a range of social media platforms. She seeks to understand where her competition is and how she can leverage her assets through a differentiation strategy by being unique. Instead of reacting to current and direct trends and needs, Vanessa purposefully explores the terrain, opportunities and long-term risks with the most up-to-date and relevant information at hand. By

continuously assessing where she is today and where she is going tomorrow, she can divide her energy between working *on* and working *in* the business.

Vanessa has set up, linked and automated her business banking, bookkeeping and accounts receivable and payable in the cloud. Her leadership approach stems from an internal self-assessment perspective and as a consequence she engages collaboratively with her staff and empowers them to work autonomously at a time suitable to them. This also means that she has no need for a vision board anymore as she already knows where she is heading and takes small and proactive steps towards her goals on a daily basis.

Vanessa is an internal leader, motivated by her purpose. Her ability to internally self-assess helps her influence the direction, growth and long-term sustainability of her business.

WORKING *IN* OR WORKING *ON*?

The difference between Peter and Vanessa is very clear. Peter is very hands-on and is stuck with the status quo because he doesn't have the time, clarity or opportunity to influence the direction, growth or long-term sustainability of his business. He is working *in* his business, but not *on* his business.

Vanessa is more hands-off in day-to-day operational activities so she has more time to gather and assess information that looks at the bigger picture and aligns with the vision of her business. She has set up her working day so she has more time to work *on* her business, applying the long-game approach.

From my own entrepreneurial background I know first-hand how important it is not to always work *in* the business but instead work *on* the business. By stepping out of your external leadership bubble and instead choosing an *internal perspective,* you can tackle the terrain, opportunities and long-term risks differently, just like Vanessa.

One of the biggest obstacles for growth as a leader is being predominantly focused *in* the business. When most of your time is spent continuously dealing with the operational aspects, it's hard to have enough creative bandwidth to be thinking about ways in which you can grow as a leader or scale your business. I have faced this dilemma a few times and so I know first-hand how tricky it can be.

The crucial point is to self-assess where you are today and spend quality time defining what the future state of your business will look like.

A way that has worked for myself and my clients is to:

- Define *your role,* not just the future employees' roles.
- Define how *your time* will be used, not just the employees' time.

- Define *your purpose* and how it is going to bring meaning and fulfilment, not just the employees' tasks.

How do you self-assess your own perspective? How do you know if you are driven by the external leadership perspective or motivated by the internal leadership perspective? This short self-assessment exercise will help you work out which perspective currently drives you.

> **Exercise: Assess your perspective (2 minutes)**
>
> - Stop for a moment and close your eyes.
> - Take three deep and slow breaths through your nose (30 seconds).
> - Open your eyes and ask yourself the following questions.
>
> **Question 1: Why and how am I doing business at the moment?**
> Reflect for 30 seconds on your thoughts, feelings and emotions about this question.
>
> **Question 2: What is stopping or blocking me from being open to doing business differently?**
> Reflect for 30 seconds on your thoughts, feelings and emotions about this question.
>
> **Question 3: How would I like others to remember my business ventures? What is my legacy?**
> Reflect for 30 seconds on your thoughts, feelings and emotions about this question.

Now let's take a look at what these questions might have revealed for you.

Question 1

What were your thoughts, feelings and emotions around how and why you are doing business? Do you feel a bit like Peter? Are you so busy just keeping up that you don't have time, clarity or opportunity to influence your business's direction, growth and long-term sustainability? If so, you are operating from the external leader perspective.

This is not surprising because our current leadership model is based around the 'doing-more-achieve' mantra, so it is likely you will relate more to Peter than Vanessa. From birth, all human beings learn through observation, mimicking others and repetition (reflective of external leadership) so it is normal to stay in this cycle as an adult.

As discussed in Part 1, achievement-oriented external leadership is the cultural norm in our society. If this is the only type of leadership you have experienced, it is near impossible for you *not* to adopt this perspective. Fiona Robertson writes in her 2020 book *Rules of Belonging* that 'culture is the rules of belonging'. She states that the need to belong to a group is so strong that it overrides most individual beliefs and values. She explains that our brains are hard-wired to belong because when we were hunter gatherers belonging was paramount to survival. So when we join the group, in this case the world of business, we will adopt whatever pattern or perspective is role-modelled to earn belonging in the group.

You can help to set a new cultural norm by adopting some of Vanessa's characteristics for doing business. This is more than simply making unrealistic commitments to yourself, this is about shifting your perspective by continuously self-assessing.

Question 2

What were your thoughts, feelings and emotions around question two? What's stopping you from being open to doing business differently? Is it fear of change? Lack of time? Being wedded to the status quo?

When the status quo entrenches your perspective it's hard to see or even have the capacity to imagine doing things differently. It is easier to remain on a steady course, content with the status quo and not rock the boat.

In his 1961 book *Normative Discourse,* American philosopher Paul W Taylor wrote that there is no point investigating the status quo of education in an attempt to discover what the purpose of education ought to be. The same analogy can be used for any organisation, there is no point investigating the status quo of an organisation in an attempt to discover its purpose. Instead, you must rigorously self-assess and decide internally what kind of organisation you wish to bring forth before you take convincing action to create this reality.

This can be explained using an iceberg as an analogy. Under the water level is your internal leader perspective, in the form of values, beliefs and assumptions that you hold. Above the water level is your external leader's perspective, in the form of your tasks, actions and behaviours. When you want to transform the status quo, you must dive under the surface, pursue your internal perspective and role-model what you wish to create.

Question 3
What were your thoughts, feelings and emotions around your legacy? If you want your business to live on, you'll need to take a leaf out of Vanessa's book and make the time and space to work *on* your business, not just *in* it. One of the first things you could do here is to identify any blind spots you may have.

THE BLIND SPOT

Kodak was so eager to hold on to film development that they never went to market with the world's first digital camera, which was invented by them. Blockbuster has gone bye-bye, most likely full of regrets because they turned down the idea of purchasing Netflix from the Netflix founders in the year 2000. Both of these businesses failed to realise the shifting landscapes in which they operated and remained with the status quo, which later came back to bite them.

Things move in years and decades now, not centuries and millennia. Your ability to purposefully explore the terrain, opportunities and long-term risks is more important today than ever before. Don't let your perspective become your blind spot!

One particular entrepreneur that I mentored over many years initially worked *in* his business. His motto was not to hire staff if he could do it himself.

His blind spot was that he thought he was saving money; he didn't realise that he was actually inhibiting growth!

Through a lot of coaching, he eventually realised that he should not waste his creative energy on the mundane, such as bookkeeping, or things he wasn't good or efficient with, such as his website or social media. Once he realised this, he was open to a new perspective. This is when I shifted to mentoring him to look for signs, risks and changing external factors that may impact his ability to grow. The more he shifted his focus to work *on* his business, the more he grew as a person and consequently his business. He is still today a very successful entrepreneur.

INFORMATION AND PERSPECTIVE

Does information shape your perspective or does your perspective shape how you take in information?

For a perspective to form, you must have access to information. If you think back to the examples at the beginning of the chapter, the information that Vanessa was looking for and working with was very different from that of Peter. Peter was so busy responding to information from within his business that he had no bandwidth to lift his gaze and look beyond the here and now. Vanessa, on the other hand, had arranged her workload in such a way that she was proactively seeking out information that would help her business grow. Peter's externally driven perspective and Vanessa's internally motivated perspective are intrinsically connected to how they seek information.

> **Perspective determines how you respond to information that comes to you. A simple example of this is the glass half full/glass half empty viewpoint. Both the optimist and the pessimist have the same information (half a glass of water), but each views it with a different perspective.**

Let's look at a couple of other examples of how people seek and respond to information.

As a HR Director, Amara seeks information from a wide range of sources. This includes reading *Harvard Business Review* articles that challenge her current HR practices, facilitating discussions with staff members, and participating in online HR forums with culturally diverse participants from across the globe. She derives meaning and purpose from information with an open mindset and invites contradictory views that challenge her and enrich conversations.

As a lending officer at one of the big four banks in Australia, Robert comes to work to perform tasks that enable loans. He seeks information from inside the bank such as current policies and procedures and reads news articles that align with his style of working. He feels there is no need to change and he rejects any information that seeks to challenge the status quo (such as information about community banking initiatives or research about fintech lenders).

The way that Amara and Robert seek and respond to information is dramatically different. Amara's perspective is far-reaching and she's open to being challenged; Robert's perspective is narrow and he only seeks information that confirms what he knows or thinks. Robert is wedded to the status quo and stuck in his perspective, while Amara is proactively creating the future.

It is important to carefully and meticulously assess the information that flows to you because the information you *accept* or *reject* will ultimately determine the strength of your connection with your internal leader.

When your connection with your internal leader is *strong* and your internal *WHO* part motivates your actions, you tend to *accept* that there are many different perspectives and you internally self-assess these perspectives before choosing an action that aligns with your internal *WHO* part.

An internal leader responsibly and respectfully asks insightful questions, makes suggestions, offers perspective, raises counterpoints and proposes alternatives. The internal leader will also ask 'reverse' questions such as, 'What do I anticipate *not* to find?' What might I dismiss too hastily and what would happen if I changed my perspective on things or events?

When your connection with your internal leader is *weak* and a task-oriented external leadership perspective drives your actions, you tend to *reject* other perspectives, as yours is the 'right' one. The purpose of your actions is to maintain the status quo.

Seeking a different perspective starts by courageously asking yourself hard-hitting and truth-seeking questions so that the process of self-assessment comes to life.

The following exercise is designed to be thought-provoking and challenging. Let curiosity stimulate your desire to ask these questions when you feel that you need a reminder about the meaning and purpose of your professional practice.

Exercise: Information self-assessment

Four hard-hitting and truth-seeking questions to ask yourself:
1. **What** kind of information brings meaning and purpose to your professional practice?
2. **Where** does the information that brings meaning and purpose to your professional practice come from?
3. **Why** does this information bring meaning and purpose to your professional practice?
4. **Who** is the bearer of this information that brings meaning and purpose to your professional practice?

Question 1: What kind of information brings meaning and purpose to your professional practice?

Self-assessment questions
1. Does the information you *currently* accept bring meaning and purpose to your professional practice?
2. Are you willing to accept that the information that you *currently* accept might be incorrect and that it no longer aligns with your purpose?
3. Are you worried that you might find that you wasted years on doing something that did not align with your internal leader?

Example
*If you are driven by your **external leader**, you tend to **reject** information that presents perspectives that challenge the status quo. Action and doing gets the job done, there is no need to stop and assess all the time; who cares if it maintains the status quo or not. You are not interested in change.*

On the contrary, if your connection with your **internal leader** is strong, the information that you tend to **accept** enriches conversations and challenges perspectives, habits and unconscious biases that maintain the status quo. You are willing to change your perspective and accept that two contradictory perspectives can co-exist.

Question 2: Where does the information that brings meaning and purpose to your professional practice come from?

Self-assessment questions
1. Have you limited the number of pathways for how information can flow to you (intentionally or unintentionally)?
2. Do you trust information that does not follow the usual information flow?
3. What do you have to gain or lose if you invite information to come from a route less travelled?

Example
*If you are **driven by your external leader** you tend to **reject** information that doesn't align with your current perspective. Instead, you seek information that confirms your perspective from avenues such as uneducated opinions and social media posts. For example, the uneducated opinion that men are better than women at running an organisation can be based on the fact that there are more male than female CEOs.*

*On the contrary, if your connection with your **internal leader** is strong, the information that you tend to **accept** seeks out avenues such as the latest independent data, research and staff feedback. You believe in facts that are backed up by reliable sources.*

Question 3: Why does this information bring meaning and purpose to your professional practice?

Self-assessment questions
1. Does this information make you feel safe?
2. Does accepting or rejecting this information require compromise?
3. Does this information escalate or de-escalate your situation?
4. Is the main reason this information comes to you to defend your position or the status quo?
5. Does the information prove you 'right'?
6. Does being 'wrong' mean that you are a failure or that you failed?

Example
If you are **driven by your external leader** you tend to **reject** self-assessment. You also tend not to care whether or not the information provides meaning and purpose to your professional practice. You seek to defend your perspective, regardless of whether your perspective provides meaning and purpose or not.

On the contrary, if your connection with your **internal leader** is strong, the information that you tend to **accept** helps you to self-assess and clearly see that your professional practice is meaningful and purposeful. With this information, you are able to competently self-assess whether or not a change of perspective is necessary.

Question 4: Who is the bearer of this information that brings meaning and purpose to your professional practice?

Self-assessment questions
1. Who pays the wage of the information-bearer?
2. What influences the wage payer's perspective?
3. Are they influenced by lobbyists, corporations or grassroots movements?
4. Do they have power or influence within the current status quo?
5. Are they short-sighted and self-interested *or* are they in it for the long game and for the betterment of all impacted parties?

Example
*If you are **driven by your external leader** you tend to **reject** information from anyone who does not serve your cause. People are either with you or against you. Their actions drive their values.*

*On the contrary, if your connection with your **internal leader** is strong, the information that you tend to **accept** comes from someone that you trust as independent and objective. They are usually interested in the betterment of all affected parties rather than a select few. Their values motivate their actions.*

Did you find yourself nit-picking at some of the examples above? Why do you think that is? Could it be that your blue pill-popping external leader feels threatened by being questioned? The above examples are simply there to nudge you to assess your perspectives and ultimately shift towards connecting with your internal leader.

You can also shift the focus of this exercise from questioning to recalling. For example:

- 'Can you **recall** a time when you invited information from a route less travelled that contradicted your position or understanding?'
- When was the last time this occurred, one week ago, three months ago, one year ago, ever?
- Why do you think that is?
- How did it make you feel?

Another recall question could be:

- 'Can you **recall** a time when information defended your position or the status quo?'
- Why did you have a need to defend your position?
- Who gained or lost from this experience?

Let's go back to the tortoise and the hare analogy. Did you find that your perspective tilted towards staying in the comfort zone that is represented by the status quo? Do you find yourself working *in* your business rather than *on* it? If you relate to this, you are more the reactive, ever-moving hare.

Did you find that you tilted more towards wanting to grow and shift your perspective through self-assessment? Do you find yourself working *on* the growth and development of your business? If you relate to this, you are more the proactive, steady-progress tortoise.

Contemplating these hard-hitting and truth-seeking questions is a form of self-assessment. As an internal leader, you must continuously self-assess so that the *what, where* and *why* of your organisation align with your unique internal *WHO* part. Your self-assessing state of mind will help shift your mindset to effortlessly attract transformational moments that fuel you rather than drain you.

CHAPTER 4
BUILDING HABITS THAT SERVE

Question: are your current habits enriching your professional practice or are they wasting opportunities and your valuable time?

REFLECTING ON YOUR HABITS

Bridget Jones's Diary, the 1996 novel by Helen Fielding, features the trials and tribulations of Bridget Jones, portrayed by Renée Zellweger in the 2001 romantic comedy with the same name. She is a young professional who is balancing work commitments with competing personal worries about her weight and her self-sabotaging habits such as excessive smoking and drinking, which she believes are stopping her from finding true love. At one point, she feels deflated but self-reflective and she starts a new job and changes her habits by going to the gym and cutting down on cigarettes and alcohol. At the end of the movie, Bridget realises that she is lovable even though she believes that she is overweight when she finds a man that likes her just the way she is.

I can personally relate to the story of Bridget Jones, as I myself was once held hostage by my distractive habits. My thoughts deceived me and I became a slave to my assumptions. Through self-reflection and taking an inventory of my habits, I broke free of my unhelpful habits and gained time that I'd previously wasted on the mundane. This extra time provided further opportunities for self-reflection, which led to further refinement of my habits and so on...

The story of Bridget Jones is the perfect segue into your own habits. If you took inventory of your habits, would you find them helpful or unhelpful? You might find that some of your habits are distractions; these habits make it feel like things happen automatically *to you*, without your direct conscious input. Other habits may be serving you well and these habits make it feel like *you* are in control. You will benefit greatly from being conscious and reflective of your habits as it will help you understand how you show up as a leader. This is why reflecting on habits is one of the elements in the leadership framework.

THE *WHAT* AND *WHO* OF HABITS

Our habits and assumptions are formed by our life experiences through a trial-and-error conditioning process, often influenced by social or cultural expectations. Habits are driven by *assumptions* that support either the external *WHAT* part or the internal *WHO* part of who we are.

Habits derived from our external *WHAT* assumptions align with what we do, such as our job, how we measure achievement and our education. In these instances, habits are formed outside of our awareness. An example of this is coping with work stressors by reactively taking a smoke break or yelling at staff. I call this being *held by our assumptions*.

Habits that are driven by internal *WHO* assumptions align with our values, such as practising compassion, being caring or connecting with our emotions. In these instances, we are aware of these habits forming. An example of this is proactively taking five minutes to be mindful during a stressful workday instead of smoking or yelling at staff. Rather than being *held by our assumptions*, we *hold our assumptions*.

What kind of leader you are is partly determined by your consistently performed habits. Habits influenced by your external *WHAT* will keep you busy and make you believe that what you do and achieve is important, which allows your actions and achievements to set the tone for your values. For example, habitually leaving meetings early because you 'don't have time to fuss with the details' sets the tone for how much (or little) you value your team. One leader I worked with habitually said yes to every request from her manager even though it wasn't part of her role; this habit devalued her and set the tone that her role can be lumped with requests even though she was already working at capacity.

This is in stark contrast to habits that are influenced by your internal WHO part where your actions and achievements are consequences of your values. For example, if you habitually greet your staff as you come into work in the morning, perhaps pausing for a chat here or there, you are acting on your value of caring. One leader I worked with knew the names and birthdays of hundreds of employees and their partners and would go out of his way to send his congratulations on their birthday; he modelled the value of connection.

THE NEED TO 'FIT IN'

Habits can also be influenced by our need to 'fit in'. Habits that help us fit in are a powerful motivator (and a huge time-wasting exercise). In an attempt to fit in, Bridget Jones worries about her weight. Society's unrealistic expectations about how a woman should look cause her to believe that she is overweight (even though she isn't). This assumption *holds* her and causes her to behave in a less beneficial way towards herself (in the movie, she seeks acceptance in her philandering boss's bed).

Society is full of visible and invisible *shoulds* and *should nots*; this is what we call culture. Culture is a pattern of basic actions, thoughts and traditions that generate belonging within a group; it is the way things are done. Within our current culture, the expected norm is to follow and to conform, without questioning or evaluating. We can form time-wasting habits to help us fit in to our society and culture, such as working through lunch break to impress your boss.

This makes it hard to challenge the status quo and build different *WHO*-driven habits, but that's exactly what we need to do if we are going to break free of our external *WHAT*-driven habits and take back some control.

MAKING AND BREAKING HABITS

You might be surprised to learn that your habits were first formed by the choices you made. Many of these choices are made outside of your awareness, and therefore you may feel you are not personally accountable for them. You may believe that your habits are simply a consequence of life circumstances beyond your control, but nothing could be further from the truth. You don't need to be held hostage by your assumptions and habits any longer.

You have the power to break old habits and make new ones. It's not easy, but it's absolutely possible.

The first step in bringing back control in your life is to reflect on your habits to see if they are serving you. Do they support you or are they distractive or self-sabotaging?

To do this it's important to understand system one and system two thinking and how they contribute to making and breaking habits.

SYSTEM ONE AND SYSTEM TWO THINKING

In his ground-breaking 2011 book *Thinking, Fast and Slow*, Daniel Kahneman explains how the brain is characterised by two systems: system one and system two. System one of your brain is the automatic, fast and intuitive system and is used to make automatic decisions; it's the brain's 'default setting'. For example, system one is engaged to answer questions like, 'What is the capital city of your home country?' or, 'What does 1 + 1 equal?'. On the other hand, system two of your brain is the rational, intellectual and logical system that involves thinking, assessing available information and evaluating what information might be missing, correct or incorrect before making a decision. For example, system two is engaged to answer the question, 'What is the capital city of Liechtenstein?' or 'What does 33 x 963 equal?' (unless you are a genius or a human calculator!)[1].

Kahneman, who is an Israeli psychologist and economist, also states that system one of your brain cannot be shut down, its

---

1. If you are curious – Vaduz is the capital of Liechtenstein, and 33 x 963 = 31,779.

most important task is to determine what the norm is in your personal world. If system one thinking perceives something that does not seem normal, system two thinking is engaged, allowing you to concentrate and be in control. Conscious choices are made based on rationality, intellect and logic.

The majority of the time, you can rely on system one thinking, even though it can be burdened by distortions and systematic errors that occur under certain circumstances. An example of such a distortion is when the repetition of an event or activity causes system one thinking to consider the event or activity as normal, leading to increased acceptance of the event or activity. For Bridget Jones, smoking and drinking are considered normal at the beginning of the movie (system one thinking). However, when life provides her some self-reflection time (system two thinking), she changes her habits and starts exercising and cuts down on cigarettes and alcohol.

Our habits are controlled by system one thinking. Even though we once made the choice to allow a habit to form, once the behaviour or pattern becomes entrenched through repetition, it becomes 'automatic'. To reflect on our habits and understand the role they play in our life, we need to engage system two thinking.

Early in my career, in a time before self-reflection had entered my world, I would take on other people's bad habits. At one stage, when I was a young chef apprentice, my system one thinking perceived yelling at the front of house staff as normal. Crazy shit! How awful it must have been for those poor front of house staff to receive my verbal abuse for not picking up the food immediately when I rang the bell. The fact that they attended to guests' other needs did not enter my underdeveloped mind.

QUESTIONING ASSUMPTIONS

Robert Kegan and Lisa Laskow Lahey wrote in their book Immunity to Change that in an effort to change your habits, you must first overcome the fear of potential fallout that this change could entail, such as disappointment or shame. To exemplify how hard it is to break free from habits, the book mentions a study where only one in seven heart patients changed their habits to save their own life (based on doctors' recommendations). Perhaps these patients were held by assumptions such as science or technology will save them, being in denial about the dangers (it will not happen to me) or that they were simply too busy, important or powerful to act on lifesaving advice from doctors. Whatever the reason, it demonstrates the power that assumptions have on our habits.

Barriers and perceived obstacles for succeeding in changing your habits are often hidden in plain sight, in *assumptions that hold you*. Bridget Jones is held by an assumption that because she is overweight, she is not loveable and this causes her to perform self-sabotaging habits. Of course, none of this is true and the movie shows this beautifully when her old childhood friend tells her he likes her just the way she is.

In order to form new habits, you need to engage your system two thinking to reflect on the *assumptions that hold you*. Do these assumptions support your external *WHAT* or your internal *WHO*? The process of self-reflection is one of the keys to personal mastery and system two thinking enables the process of self-reflection as you think, assess and evaluate before jumping into action and drawing conclusions. Paradoxically, you might end up having a system one habit that automatically self-reflects (system two)!

Bridget Jones's transition from being held hostage by distracting and self-sabotaging habits (system one) to being supported by self-reflective habits that serve her (system two) is a wonderful illustration of her growth as a person. As a result of taking inventory of her situation and questioning her assumptions, she starts a new job where she feels valued. Her professional practice, as well as her personal life, are enriched by a different set of habits. Do you find yourself wondering how she achieved such change? You will find the answers in Chapter 6 – Transforming your Internal Library, where we explore how, why and where behaviours originate from.

ASCENDING THE FIVE-STEP STAIRCASE

When system two thinking is engaged, you are able to reflect on your existing, automatic habits. When you are in this self-reflective state, you can form more intentional habits that serve you and begin heading towards the north end of leadership. I call this iterative approach to building habits the personal, continuous improvement framework. You will come to understand this name once you ascend the staircase. I have created a five-step exercise to guide you through this process. The steps are:

1. Take inventory of your current habits relating to work.
2. Based on your inventory, decide on a goal for change.
3. Recognise assumptions that are getting in the way of your goal.
4. Identify and act on steps that are needed to accomplish your goal.
5. Reward and reflect, please return to step one.

I'll walk you through each of these steps as we go.

> ### Exercise: Ascending the five-step staircase
>
> Imagine that you are on the ground floor and you are about to ascend a flight of stairs to the first floor.
>
> You take **the first step** and you see a sign with small green letters that reads, '*Take inventory* **of your current habits relating to work**'. As an example, let's begin by tracking your habits for a working week.
>
> How many of your current habits are enriching your professional practice? Maybe you are not sure or you are confused about your habits. To clarify, ask yourself if your habits are driven by your external *WHAT* or your internal *WHO*? The important thing at this step is that you are honest with yourself. Use this tool to help you.

Take inventory – a tool to track your habits

I have provided some examples to kick-start your system two, self-reflective thinking of your habits. I want to highlight that externally driven habits can still enrich your professional practice and all aren't 'bad'!

Current habit	External *WHAT* part driven – Yes or No	Internal *WHO* part driven – Yes or No	Enriching your professional practice – Yes or No	Assumption
Spend time supporting co-workers.	No	Yes	Yes	I *hold* the assumption that empathy is important.
Creating new systems and ways to increase sales in the business.	Yes	No	Yes	I am *held by* the assumption that the number of sales is relative to my worth.
Trying to fit in at work so you can get the next promotion.	Yes	No	No	I am *held by* the assumption that fitting in is more important than following my own values.
Saying yes to every request from your manager.	Yes	No	No	I am *held by* the assumption that my manager's request is more important than my current job role.

| Work overtime. | Yes | No | No | I am *held by* the assumption that my level of commitment to my job is measured by how many hours I work. |

You take a **second step** and spot another sign, this one with amber letters that reads, '**Based on your inventory, decide on a goal for change**'.

Let's draw from an example in the table above. You decide to change the habit of saying yes to every request from your manager. You set a goal that you want to say no to unreasonable requests, especially when you are already at maximum capacity. This is a very reasonable goal to have, yet you may feel uneasy or unsafe standing up for yourself in such a way, especially against an authority figure.

You take a **third step** and find another sign with blue letters that ask you to, '**Recognise assumptions that are getting in the way of your goal**'.

If this goal makes you feel uneasy or unsafe, it is most likely your assumptions whispering in your ear. In the table, I've suggested that the assumption you hold is that the manager's request is more important than your current job tasks. By creating the goal, you are challenging this assumption and the devil on your shoulder. By self-reflecting and recognising this assumption, you slowly break free from its grip.

Another example is a person who wants to stop working overtime and spend more time with their family. This person is held by the assumption that their commitment to work is measured by the number of hours worked. They fear being viewed as lazy or uncommitted due to this assumption.

An assumption that held me in the past was the fear of not being enough. To avoid challenging this assumption, I used an external task-oriented approach as a leader and focused on results rather than self-reflection.

What assumptions and behaviours are distracting or blocking you from your goal? Working through this is probably the biggest task of this exercise, so don't rush this one. It can take some deep reflection to recognise and understand what assumptions are holding you.

Step four has a window that looks over green pastures and someone has used a ride-on mower to write the following message on the lawn, '**Identify and act on steps that are needed to accomplish your goal**'.

The key to building new habits is to intentionally and sincerely attach a small, clear and attainable step to your goal. This often requires testing phases because it's hard to plan what steps will support your goal.

Small, attainable steps will make it feel like you are constantly accomplishing and getting closer to your main goal.

Let's go back to the example of saying no to your manager and unpack a few steps to help move towards the goal. You may share your calendar with your manager to illustrate your workload. You could email progress reports to your manager that outline issues and risks that you are currently solving. If you're feeling bold, as a response to a request from your manager, you could ask them which of your current jobs they wish to delay while you handle their request. It is fascinating how effective this bold strategy is. It has personally worked for me *many* times!

Bridget Jones's approach was to get another job and change her habits; she was intentional and sincere with this undertaking and therefore succeeded. What steps would work for you? For example, if your goal is to get more self-reflection time between meetings, what steps could you take? One suggestion could be to only book 45-minute meetings per hour, rather than 60-minute meetings back-to-back. I personally allocate time in my calendar to 'undertake my job role' where I focus solely on strategic thinking and finalising tasks. This challenges my assumption that in order to be productive I have to be in a meeting with my colleagues.

Step five takes you up to the first floor and you receive a certificate with golden letters saying, '**Reward and reflect, please return to step one**'.
First of all, congratulations, you now know how to build habits that serve you! But it's not enough to know how to build habits, even though this step deserves the biggest reward. The real success lies within sustaining these habits by activating system two thinking and reflecting on whether or not these habits are serving you tomorrow and beyond. I therefore urge you to continuously return to step one in a perpetual loop of building habits that serve.

> This iterative approach to building habits that serve is your personal continuous improvement framework. Habits, and the routines built around these habits, support the big goals in life and who you want to become. Who you are and who you become is determined by you, not anyone else.

FROM LITTLE THINGS...

This invitation for you to take inventory of your current habits and determine which ones are useful and which ones are better left behind will help you take back control of how you spend your time, one iteration at a time! It is a rigorous reminder of the power behind little things in life called habits. Don't be hard on yourself if you do not succeed at first. Rest assured that practice makes progress, even if it feels slow at first. To quote Australian singer-songwriters Kev Carmody and Paul Kelly, 'from little things big things grow'!

Habits that are driven by your external *WHAT* part will keep you busy by doing more and achieving more, but to what end?

External achievements are important, but in the big scheme of things, are they really more important than you becoming compassionate, caring or more connected with your emotions?

External achievements might appear to bring improvement to your professional practice in the form of promotions or wage increases. Unfortunately, these external achievements will do little to enrich your professional practice. By contrast, habits that are driven by your internal *WHO* part will vastly enrich your professional practice as they stem from self-reflection.

The *WHAT* part measures progress with numbers and job titles. Life is a constant race against the clock and what you are doing is more important than who you are becoming. You might even feel guilty if you slow down, take a breath and just enjoy the moment. The irony is that unless you stop for a moment and self-reflect, your actions might set the tone for your values. Actions that are consequences of your values stem from your *WHO* part, and connecting with your *WHO* part requires time and effort. This time is available to you if you choose to stop for a moment and reflect on your habits and I hope the tools in this book enable you to do so.

When your habits are formed from the *WHO* part, your goals look very different; they are less externally achievement-focused. When time is your ally, you can engage system two thinking, reflect on your current habits and connect with your *WHO* part. This internal self-reflection supports your progression towards self-regulation and personal mastery.

CHAPTER 5

CHALLENGING UNCONSCIOUS BIAS

Question: are you aware of how your unconscious bias affects your behaviour as a leader?

THE IMPACT OF UNCONSCIOUS BIAS

As a young manager, I truly believed that I was above average and knew more than most. By occupying as much space as possible, I would skew data in my favour and argue profusely in an attempt to appear knowledgeable in front of others. I devoted a lot of time and effort to protecting and highlighting my self-image. I would blame staff and other external factors for anything that didn't shine a bright light on my stardom.

I couldn't trust staff as they appeared far too relaxed and lazy compared to the professionalism that I believed I role-modelled. How could I possibly trust staff who portrayed such poor character? Through my managerial lens, their input often consisted of slacking off and joking around when they should have been working and this caused me to double and triple check everything they did. The staff's lack of compliance with my management rules led me to develop resentment towards the staff under my care.

My lack of self-awareness and understanding of the impact of my behaviour eventually had catastrophic consequences ranging from staff not contributing in meetings to declining staff retention. There were a number of factors contributing to my warped ideas about what leadership is and how to manage effectively, but the key factor I want to explore here is the damaging effects of my unconscious biases.

WE ALL HAVE UNCONSCIOUS BIAS

You may have heard of the conundrum 'the surgeon's dilemma'. A boy and his father are involved in a terrible car accident. Tragically, the father dies on the scene and the boy is rushed to hospital. The boy is wheeled into emergency surgery and the surgeon says, 'I can't operate on this patient, he's my son.' How can that be?

The answer of course, is that the surgeon is the boy's mother. Those who struggle to solve the puzzle are being blinkered by their assumption that the surgeon is male. This is their unconscious bias at work.

Unconscious bias is the master of snap judgments so that more brainpower is freed up to perform more complex tasks. Unconscious bias doesn't care who gets hurt, it supports the function of collating massive amounts of information and presenting this information to you in a way that has made sense to you in the past. This automatic process happens every moment of the day, so there is a high reliance on familiar shortcuts to speed up the process. As a south-dweller, these automatic snap judgements and familiar shortcuts are not equipped to be reflective, compassionate or tolerant, often resulting in devastating judgments. As a north-sider that has practiced self-reflection, these automatic snap judgements and shortcuts may stem from a more compassionate mindset, resulting in more tolerant judgements.

Exercise: Exploring your unconscious bias

If I ask you to close your eyes and picture a carpenter what comes to mind?

Sex	female	male	other
Age	18–30	31–60	61–100
Relationship status	single	married/de facto	divorced
Complexion	dark	tanned	fair
Religion	religious	non-religious	other
Political leaning	right	left	neutral
Physicality	strong	weak	neutral
Smoker?	smoker	never smoked	former smoker
Vehicle they drive	small, car	ute/truck	van

The image in your mind is mostly constructed by your unconscious bias. One of the first valuable steps in challenging our unconscious bias is to be aware that it constantly fills in the gaps in our environment. The result of the exercise is to make you aware of the subtleties of unconscious bias and how it affects every one of your thoughts and decisions.

Being aware of unconscious bias does not necessarily stop it but enables you to make allowances for decisions and behaviours that would otherwise go unnoticed.

Once you are aware of how unconscious bias affects thinking, you can begin to understand how you and others 'tick'.

This helps you to understand why somebody might act a certain way, not only on the surface through their behaviour, but also at a deeper level that stems from their beliefs and values.

I like to imagine the power of unconscious bias as riding on the back of a gigantic, starving T-Rex that is chasing down an afternoon snack. Who is in control, you or the T-Rex? I think we both know the answer! Aside from the T-Rex analogy, there is a wealth of academic research around unconscious bias. In fact, I find this area so fascinating and vital to my work as a leadership mentor that I studied it during my Master's research project.

TEN TYPES OF UNCONSCIOUS BIAS

Unconscious bias comes in numerous forms. Firstly, unconscious bias can be either against or towards someone or something. For example:

You **don't like** male managers = you have a bias **against** male managers.

You **like** male managers = you have a bias **towards** male managers.

Beyond this, unconscious bias can manifest itself in many ways. I've listed just ten of them here to get you started. Perhaps you can spot your runaway T-Rex in some of them?

1. The above-average effect

The above-average effect, also known as illusory superiority, describes how the majority of people tend to believe that they are above average in a range of skills. For example, if you ask any driver and they will most likely tell you that they are an above-average driver even though that defies both logic and statistical probability. If every driver is above average, then this becomes the new average. A 1981 study by Ola Svenson found this attitude to be a common phenomenon.

2. Affinity bias

When leaders and organisations hire or promote based on 'cultural fit', they are most likely affected by affinity bias; a natural liking for someone. A person with this bias attempts to hire or promote based on who they think they will get along with. Instead of hiring a 'cultural fit', how would it look if we hired based on 'cultural add'? Some of the possible consequences of affinity bias in an organisation include a lack of crucial perspectives and competencies and a wide range of experiences in staff.

3. Ageism

Many organisations have an age discrimination bias against the mature workforce as well as the younger generations. This bias may perceive mature workers as slow learners that are stuck in their ways. On the flip side, ageism may paint young people as lazy or lacking in loyalty because they frequently change jobs. Ageism can also be seen in the language and the tech skills requirements that are used in job advertisements. My personal favourite is only hiring a 'digital native' – someone that has grown up with new technologies rather than from the mature workforce.

4. Confirmation bias

A person with this cognitive bias tends to look for information that champions their belief or bias. This bias also leads to an enhanced and biased recall of memories. When you suffer from confirmation bias, any interpretation of information that is contrary to yours is ignored; data and results are often statistically skewed when this bias is present. If you are suffering from confirmation bias you often lack depth and perspective in discussions. In strategic thinking, confirmation bias leads to shallow and narrow goals and outcomes. An example is a manager who believes that female employees are unreliable. A new female employee of this manager runs late on three occasions in her first month due to accidents on the road she takes to work. Regardless of the reason, her manager's bias is 'confirmed' and they continue to believe that female employees are unreliable.

5. Fundamental attribution error

This is when an individual attributes somebody else's circumstances or mistakes to their character or mood. For example, if a colleague always runs late for meetings, you might decide (you perceive) this is because they are lazy or nonchalant (personal factors). On the contrary, *you* blame external factors for personally being late to meetings such as, it was raining, a lack of parking or the train was running late.

6. Gender bias

This is the invisible 'rule' that determines how one should act or what job one should have based on gender. In the western world, it often begins at birth with pink clothes and dolls for girls and blue clothes and cars for boys. In adulthood, these rules translate themselves into problematic truths such as males are better managers, CEOs, engineers and doctors. Women, on the other hand, are better teachers, nurses, secretaries or stay-at-home parents. Of course, none of this is true.

7. Halo and horns effect

This bias lets the first impression of someone dictate a biased positive or negative opinion of someone. The halo bias may perceive someone as competent based on their looks or the name of the university they attended. The horns bias may perceive someone as negative or incompetent based on their height, eye colour, the car they drive or the suburb they live in. For example, if you've had a previous altercation in the workplace with somebody named Peter, you may be less likely to hire another Peter in the future due to the horns effect.

8. Height bias

I imagine somebody making up the perfect concoction for a CEO. 'Ah yes, a dash of white, must be male, and let's add a splash of height for good measure – at least 6 feet tall!'. In Malcolm Gladwell's 2006 book *Blink*, he sampled 50% of the companies on the Fortune 500 list and found that on average CEOs are about six feet tall (approximately 181 cm). Compared to the average height of American males, CEOs are on average a staggering three inches taller (approximately 7.6 cm). If you think height doesn't matter, think again, and think T-Rex!

Further to this, did you know that for women, every centimetre of height will increase their chance of being a leader? A 2019 European study by Felix Bittmann found this to be true. Are the leaders in your organisation tall or short?

9. Prejudice

This bias is a negative attitude towards a particular cohort of people or individual members of the cohort. Stereotyping or overgeneralisation of a particular group or its members is not based on fact but rather on behaviour derived from sets of beliefs that trigger negative feelings. In an organisation, this may be prevalent in a lack of cultural diversity due to prejudice against different cultures and religions.

10. Self-serving bias

This is the tendency for an individual to take credit for positive outcomes, such as achievements or competencies, but blame external factors for negative outcomes such as failures or disappointing events. Self-serving bias is considered a way of protecting and improving one's self-image. An example of this is attributing a high monthly sales report to you being a skilled sales associate, and a low monthly sales report on a lack of customers coming through the business.

> **Exercise: Spot the T-Rex**
>
> Read back over this chapter's opening story of my former self as an ineffective and controlling manager. See if you can identify where these three unconscious biases were at play:
> - above-average effect
> - fundamental attribution error
> - self-serving bias.
>
> I'll be waiting for you here with the answers. (No cheating!)

...

Welcome back. Now let's see how you went. These are my answers; maybe you came up with something I've missed.

Above-average effect: *As a young manager, I truly believed that I was an above-average manager who knew more than most.*

Fundamental attribution error: *They appeared far too relaxed and lazy compared to the professionalism that I believed I role-modelled. How could I possibly trust staff who portrayed such poor character?*

Self-serving bias: *I would blame staff and other external factors for anything that didn't shine a bright light on my stardom.*

MY D.B.I.J. DEFENCE MECHANISM

As that young, immature leader, I developed a repertoire of staged defence mechanisms to fend off attacks against my unconscious biases: denial, blame, ignorance and justification (D.B.I.J.).

Stage 1: Denial
I was in denial of my staff's abilities to contribute to the team and believed I was above them, denying any gaps in my own abilities.

Stage 2: Blame
When things didn't go my way, I would blame my staff and other external factors rather than taking responsibility for my own actions.

Stage 3: Ignorance
I was ignorant of the effects that my micromanaging had on my staff's confidence in themselves to perform tasks.

Stage 4: Justification
I justified my fundamental attribution error by perceiving my team's relaxed attitude as them being unprofessional and lazy.

Back then, my lack of self-awareness stopped me from realising how empty my professional life was. I was caught up in all the blame and denial that controlled my choices. I pushed away people who mattered and attracted those equally as imprisoned by the D.B.I.J. defence mechanism as myself. My professional life was just a hot pot filled with ignorant and unaware people feeding off each other.

I often bring the D.B.I.J. defence mechanism into conversations with clients by phrasing each stage as a question. For example, 'After listening to the story you just shared with me, how do you think your actions affected other impacted parties?' The client's system one thinking often goes into overdrive here and all they can muster up is, 'not sure' or 'I don't know'. My follow-on question is generally, 'Are you happy to explore this with me?', which usually opens up the conversation.

If my story resonates with you, ask yourself the question: how often does my first line of defence include denial or blame?

This can be a powerful start in your journey towards self-awareness.

THE DUNNING-KRUGER EFFECT

We will now leave all the other unconscious biases behind and concentrate on one in particular, the Dunning-Kruger Effect. My Master's research project was on the Dunning-Kruger Effect and how it can impact the recruitment process in an organisation. The findings in this research were extraordinary to say the least! So why is the Dunning-Kruger Effect so interesting?

Well, keep reading and you'll soon find out for yourself.

The Dunning-Kruger Effect has been defined as the curse of the incompetent, leading to grossly optimistic self-awareness. The Dunning-Kruger Effect is a cognitive bias that sits in the field of psychology. It portrays how a person's ignorance deprives them of their ability to be self-aware, leading to inflated confidence rather than inflated competence. In their 1999 research, Dunning and Kruger found that individuals in the lowest quartile in the given field overestimated their competence by 50 percentile points.

Ignorance and inflated confidence lead to deeper and more warped bias, prejudice and perceived privilege.

When someone suffers from the Dunning-Kruger Effect, their incompetence treats rational, objective and logical facts as a foreign language.

If you suffer from the Dunning-Kruger Effect, you are unfortunately double cursed. This suffering causes you to inaccurately assess your competence (curse 1), which can lead to disastrous choices and consequences. Unfortunately, you also lack the cognitive ability to grasp this fact (curse 2), which is why the objective facts or feedback presented to you are incomprehensible.

As a young manager, I suffered from the Dunning-Kruger Effect. I overestimated my competence as a leader but was oblivious to the havoc I was wreaking in my professional career and the impact my actions had on others.

For some bonus reading, search the web for 'Dunning-Kruger Effect Curve' and you'll get a great picture that summarises the Dunning-Kruger Effect.

An incompetent person begins on the Peak of Mt Stupid, and once realising where they stand, falls down into the Valley of Despair before ascending the Slope of Enlightenment towards competence. Once you accept that you have been 'Dunning-Krugered', you can begin your journey towards competence!

Micromanaging and staff discontentment

The Dunning-Kruger Effect explains why some people with relatively low competence believe that they 'know it all' in the workplace. Because these individuals believe they know everything, they concentrate their efforts on micromanaging subordinates' tasks rather than the results from these tasks. This leads to a lack of trust and discontentment among staff. From my perspective, micromanaging tasks decreases efficiency and productivity, creating a less than perfect environment for an organisation to thrive, execute its mission and grow its financial capabilities. (For the record, micromanagement is the opposite of empowerment, which often sees organisations flourish and grow their capabilities exponentially.)

How do you think a manager suffering from the Dunning-Kruger Effect would impact an organisation? What effect would this have on staff turnover, absentees, engagement and morale? Now that you've reflected, do you think that you suffer mild symptoms of the Dunning-Kruger Effect as a leader?

I'd be shocked to meet somebody that says they've never met or worked with a micromanager. I can sniff out a micromanager from two rooms away. Why? Because I used to be one. Do you think you can sniff out a micromanager? *Just know, it takes one to know one!*

Entrenched in our culture

The Dunning-Kruger Effect is in the very fibre of our culture, society and humanity as a whole, and is especially potent in many organisations and government departments. It imprisons us and causes us to express habitual and entrenched behaviours that often negatively affect others. We justify our behaviours based on our distorted and limited thoughts.

An organisation's performance appraisal is a perfect example of the detrimental effects the Dunning-Kruger Effect can have on employees. The idea of performance appraisal is that the continuation, development and success of the organisation is based on the employees' commitment, motivation and competence. Performance appraisal interviews *should* be based on how the employees can and should contribute to the organisation. It helps shift the focus from everyday tasks to the future of the organisation. Unfortunately, the disastrous truth is that the accuracy of the performance appraisal is proportional to the level of self-awareness of the senior colleague performing it. The effect of this proportional truth is not only devastating for the individual being appraised but also for the longevity of the organisation.

Your attitudes and behaviours as a leader set the benchmark for the rest of the team.

If a leader goes into a performance appraisal sitting on the Peak of Mt Stupid and is unable to assess their *own* competence, how can they possibly assess the competence of their employees?

The leader's lack of self-awareness would impact the outcomes of these performance appraisals in ways that are flawed at best and dysfunctional at worst. How effective, accurate and objective do you think these performance appraisals are going to be?

GLASS CEILINGS AND INSTITUTIONAL BIAS

When an organisational culture develops institutional bias, it is usually invisible at first, perhaps even the norm of society at the time of its inception. Institutional bias is an inherent tendency to exclude a particular group of people through policies and procedures in a workplace. An example of this is a business not having wheelchair accessibility to and through the building. The same business may also have an institutional bias where a person with a wheelchair is not even considered for a role. The effect of such an institutional bias can be seen in fixed height workstations and out-of-reach positioning of equipment.

Another example of institutional bias is the invisible glass ceiling for women. This 'invisible glass ceiling' prevents women from reaching certain levels of senior management or executive positions because of their gender; this ceiling does not currently exist for most men in society. This bias continues to be a rampant institutional bias upheld by lesser men with little awareness of themselves – true south-dwelling behaviour. When these patterns of behaviour, that are rooted in institutional bias, slowly develop within an organisation, the organisation eventually becomes a toxic wasteland of inefficiency. This behaviour is also tremendously detrimental to equality, and if left unchecked, an organisation will spiral downwards until it can no longer survive in a competitive marketplace.

Exercise: Challenge your unconscious bias

I've designed two self-awareness exercises that will support you as a leader as you engage a self-aware state of mind and challenge your unconscious bias, and have supplied some information about a third that you can find online, which may also be helpful.

1. Substitution

Let's use an example to explain 'substitution'. Hayden doesn't like Georgiana because of her cultural background and thinks she is too loud for the workplace. He often huffs in annoyance whenever she makes a mistake. Put yourself in Hayden's shoes and ask yourself these three questions:

How would Hayden feel if Georgiana was substituted for another person (e.g. his best friend at work)?
- Do you think Hayden's behaviour would be the same towards this substitute person?
- Do you think Hayden would respond differently if this substitute person made a mistake?

Substituting the person Hayden has an unconscious bias against (Georgiana) with another person that he likes (his best friend) helps him acknowledge that there is an underlying problem *with him*, not Georgiana.

We can apply this exact same model to you. For example, if someone you don't like at work makes a mistake, you'll probably make a big deal about it and respond with anger or annoyance. If your good friend at work makes the same mistake, you probably wouldn't behave or respond the same way, but rather with empathy or humour.

Once you establish that the problem lies with *you*, there is no room for denial, blame, ignorance or justification (D.B.I.J.) anymore. It is up to *you* to challenge your unconscious bias with the help of these three self-awareness exercises!

2. Internal feedback assessment

Internal feedback can help you increase your level of self-awareness. Of course, this is a paradox, as for you to be able to recognise your own unconscious bias, you need to be aware of it, which no longer renders it unconscious! Be prepared for the long fall down Mt Stupid. The internal feedback exercise below is something that you can do individually in your own time. There is no need to share it with someone else as the intention is for you to be self-aware of your thoughts. Of course, if you wish to share the exercise results with others you are welcome to. Who knows, it might start a conversation that will help all of you to reach a deeper understanding of institutional bias, the Dunning-Kruger Effect and performance appraisals!

Part A: Name your trusted advisors board

If you had an issue or a problem you wanted to discuss, who would you go to? Make a list with three names from work and three names from outside work that you trust to bring this up with. These people could be your boss, favourite co-worker, parent or best friend. For whoever you choose, these people make up your trusted advisors board.

People at work
1.
2.
3.
People outside of work
1.
2.
3.

Part B: Add information about them

Now that you have the six names the next part of the exercise is to add in some information about them. Transfer your chosen names into the matrix below and add a note to the different columns.

- What is their sex?
- What is their age?
- What is their relationship status?
- What do they identify as their ethnic background?
- What is their religion?
- What is their political inclination?
- What is their sexual orientation?
- What is their level of education?
- Do they have access to a car?
- Do they smoke?
- Do they consume alcohol?
- Do they exercise regularly?

CHALLENGING UNCONSCIOUS BIAS

People at work	Person 1	Person 2	Person 3
Sex			
Age			
Relationship			
Ethnicity			
Religion			
Political			
Sexuality			
Education			
Car			
Smoke			
Alcohol			
Exercise			

People outside work	Person 1	Person 2	Person 3
Sex			
Age			
Relationship			
Ethnicity			
Religion			
Political			
Sexuality			
Education			
Car			
Smoke			
Alcohol			
Exercise			

Part C. Look for the trends

Is there diversity in your matrix? What surprised you most about this exercise? Can you spot your unconscious bias in the matrix? For example, do most people on your board fit in the same age bracket, drive a car or consume alcohol? This self-awareness exercise is just one way for you to start to understand the depth of your unconscious bias. It is neither right nor wrong, it is simply where you are today! From here, you can continue to challenge your unconscious bias and take active steps to change these biases.

3. Implicit association test

Here is a bonus self-awareness exercise thrown in for good measure.

In psychology, implicit behaviours refer to behaviours that happen internally, like emotional reactions and a 'train of thought'. These behaviours cannot be directly observed so it can be difficult to identify them within yourself and others. Things in our environment, like unconscious biases being triggered, signal our brains to perform these implicit behaviours. For example, you hear a group of men arguing loudly in the breakroom and you immediately feel unsafe and scared.

An implicit association test seeks to detect and measure your underlying responses and assumptions. If you search the web for the '*Harvard implicit association test*', you will find a very interesting test for unconscious bias (free of charge). By taking this test in particular, you are also contributing to important research about unconscious biases. Who knows, the test might even reveal your mightiest T-Rex!

WHEN THE PENNY DROPPED - CASE STUDY

Let me tell you a story about a client I worked with. When I first met Farima, she suffered unknowingly from the above-average effect. The D.B.I.J. defence mechanism stopped her from realising the truth about her bias. Farima measured her best qualities and strengths against someone's worst qualities and weaknesses and concluded that she was superior. One technique I used with Farima was that I asked her to close her eyes and visualise her best friend. We did exercise number one together (the example with Hayden and Georgiana) and substituted in her best friend. I knew instantly when the penny dropped and Farima realised for the first time how her biases had warped her worldview.

CHAPTER 6

TRANSFORMING YOUR INTERNAL LIBRARY

Question: Do you know what's driving your choices and behaviour? Are you a passive or an active choice architect of your own life?

YOUR CHOICES ARE DRIVEN BY YOUR INTERNAL LIBRARY

I once mentored an entrepreneur named Jasmin. In the beginning, Jasmin only had a few employees. Because of her hard work and dedication over many years, her business was booming and she now employs 30 staff in a hierarchical system of management. Even though she employs several team leaders and managers and is making a healthy profit, she is busier than ever and spends more time at work than at home.

She often feels guilty that her family is put second but she needs to manage the employees and oversee the business. Jasmin built her business from nothing, put in endless hours and sacrificed a lot of time and is not prepared to lose it. She loves her business but has this uneasy feeling deep inside that trouble is looming on the home front. When I started mentoring her, she had put her uneasy feelings aside for too long in hope that they would eventually go away.

The above case study is not rare by any account. Many people I connect with feel guilty for their choices and behaviours relating to their work. What often triggers the guilt is the perceived obligation that being at work is more valuable and important than being at home. This may be contrary to the fact that the feeling in every fibre in the body conveys a different priority and choice.

This perceived obligation is related to what I call our internal library.

Our internal library holds the books of our deep-seated beliefs, values, traditions and memories that we draw from; this library influences our behaviour and choices, often unconsciously.

The books in your internal library govern your professional practice. These books are filled with past thoughts, actions and interactions. The content of the books is influenced by a range of factors such as our perspective, habits and unconscious bias, as well as our beliefs, values, traditions and memories. It is further challenged by your sense of worth, cultural and social belonging, and environmental conditions.

Let's dig a little deeper to see the cyclical effects of these influences.

Beliefs

Beliefs are ideas that we accept as true and often without proof. Examples of this are that leadership should be solely measured by what is externally achieved, or that the truest measure of success is financial success.

Values

Our values are greatly influenced by our beliefs. Our values are the principles or standards of behaviours that we consider important. For example, you hold the belief that trusting relationships are important and therefore your interactions with others are rooted in values such as accountability and responsibility.

Traditions

Traditions are formed when beliefs and values are transmitted through generations. When a tradition is performed in the present day, it becomes a feedback loop that strengthens the idea that a particular belief is true. Traditions can have both positive and negative effects on culture and society. It could be a tradition at a workplace to celebrate each Friday afternoon with alcoholic drinks. This tradition strengthens the bond between the drinking co-workers and ostracises the non-drinking co-workers.

Memories
Memories are the cover of the books that hold our beliefs, values and traditions. Our memories are highly susceptible to distortion when emotions are attached to them. We are more likely to remember intensely happy or sad memories rather than what we ate for lunch last Wednesday.

Beliefs influence our values.

Values influence our traditions.

Traditions influence our beliefs.

Our memories are defined by this delicate and interconnecting loop.

THE TWO-WAY RELATIONSHIP WITH CHOICE AND OUR INTERNAL LIBRARY

Our internal library is related to choice in two ways. Not only does it influence the choices we make, but it is also a result of choices we once made. As you go about your day, you are constantly flicking through the pages of your books to guide your experience with your environment. Consequently, your beliefs, values, traditions and memories guide your experiences. The books that you commonly flick through may feel out of your control, or that they have been chosen for you. However, these books have been either rejected or accepted by you at some point. You are ultimately responsible for the content of your internal library.

The important lesson here is that the content that fills the books of your internal library is not necessarily true, it is simply one version of the truth. For example, Jasmin's belief that work was intrinsically more important than home life is not a universal truth, it's one she's chosen at some point. It may have been modelled by her parents (belief and memory), or she may have adopted it to counter social pressures on women to prioritise home life over work (values and tradition). Either way, it's been her choice to adopt it, which means she also has the choice to change it.

The content of your internal library is not set in stone, you can shred any books that no longer serve you at any moment in time.

This is important to realise because your ability to blossom as a unique being is intrinsically linked to the content of your internal library. So if the current content is restricting or negatively dictating your choices in your work life, it is time to evaluate and update it so it can best serve you in your professional practice.

WHAT'S IN YOUR LIBRARY?

Your internal library is the foundation of your life, including your professional life. How do you know what books fill your internal library? How would you know if a belief on a page that you have held on to for years or even decades still serves you? Perhaps your belief is hurting you or others, even if it's unintentional.

For example, holding the belief that you are not worthy enough is an example of a harmful belief – definitely a book to shred!

Let's look at two very different leaders. How do you think their beliefs, values and traditions affect their leadership style and other impacted parties? What's your gut feeling about each of them?

Leader A:

- I believe that life is a competition.
- I value feeling more important than others (egocentric).
- I follow the tradition of maximising profit and reducing the tax burden. It's okay to use tax loopholes or set up a company post box in a tax haven.

Leader B:

- I believe that honesty is the key to life.
- I value compassion in my leadership style.
- I follow the tradition of reducing the tax burden by investing in my employees and their professional development.

Your internal library will determine what you deem acceptable and not acceptable in regard to these two leaders. This boundary, between acceptable and not acceptable, is shaped by the books of your internal library.

Exercise: Discover what's in your library

Here is a three-part exercise to help you discover what books are in your internal library. By performing these exercises, you may find that some books in your internal library waste your time. Other books may challenge your view of yourself. Some books align perfectly with who you are and want to be.

1. Follow the money

After your weekly living expenses are met, what do you spend your money on? For most people, money is a limited resource. How you use money is a great insight into what books fill your internal library.

Write down the top three things you spend your money on (beyond weekly living expenses). Next to each of these things, write down what belief or value corresponds to it. Your money is spent on things that align with your internal library. Think of each item you write down like pages in a book.

For example:

Spending item	Belief or value
Yoga classes	Self-care
Education	Life-long learning
Travelling	Adventure
Partying	Socialising
Smoking	Relaxation
Savings	Security

2. Mirror, mirror on the wall...

Looking at others is like looking into a mirror, you can often only see in others what you see in yourself. What you criticise somebody for is often something you yourself are insecure about. Once you are aware of your internal library's books, you can also become aware of the books in others' internal libraries.

Write down the names of three people that you admire or wish to meet. Next to each name, write down the beliefs, values or qualities that appeal to you in these people. You will find that those you choose will often share similar books with your internal library.

For example:

Person	Belief or value or quality
Person A	Their commitment to innovation
Person B	Demonstrates empathetic leadership
Person C	Caring and attentive
Person D	Super-rich
Person E	Fearless
Person F	Has power and authority

3. What is the label?

The labels you put on yourself and others are reflected by the books in your internal library. Labels can be positive or negative, such as 'I am loyal' or 'I am careless'. Some labels, like 'I am an imposter', may stem from old, dusty books that are kept alive with the power of memories. When you become aware and connect with your labels, you also connect with the books in your internal library. When you are aware of where these labels stem from, it is easier to show empathy and keep judgements to yourself.

Write down three labels you apply to yourself and three labels that apply to someone else.

For example:

Person	Label
Me	Leads by example
Me	Full of integrity
Me	Procrastinator
Person X	Hardworking
Person X	Slow to act
Person X	Great presenter

Based on the labels you just wrote down, here are some questions to ask yourself:

1. Are the labels positive or negative?

2. What books do these labels come from? Do these labels you give yourself or others come from pages filled by your parents, social and cultural factors, or by you?

3. Reflect on the labels and ask yourself if they still resonate with you. For example, could you reframe the label 'slow to act', which has a negative connotation, to 'reflective', which is positive?

4. Do the labels that you assigned yourself or the other person limit or waste time and opportunities? Remembering that you can often only see in others what you see in yourself (from the 'mirror, mirror on the wall' exercise). For example, does being a 'procrastinator' limit you from fulfilling your potential? Does 'working hard' make you waste time on unfulfilling tasks as you chase after the unattainable pot of gold at the end of the rainbow?

5. If you could, which labels would you change? Which pages would these new labels stem from?

DECLUTTER THE LIBRARY

Now that you know how to identify the books in your internal library, it is time to declutter. If you are still strongly settled in the south, you may not believe that your internal library needs decluttering at this point in time – that's no problem. However, when you're ready to make the move to the north-side, the following exercise will help you shred any books or pages that no longer serve you.

> ### Exercise: Three steps to declutter your internal library
>
> This three-step exercise will declutter your internal library and guide you as you *assess*, *reflect* and *become aware of* your books.
>
> #### Step One – Self-assessment (perspective)
> The books you flick through to guide your experience with your environment reflect your current perspective. To explore this, you may find it useful to assess the books in your internal library using the questions below. You could also go back and reflect on the information self-assessment exercise you did in Chapter 3.
>
> *Questions*
> - Assess which books you draw from in your professional practice; does the content of these books affect your practice positively or negatively?
> - Does the content of the books narrow or widen your leadership perspective?

- Is the content of these books serving **you** as a leader or someone else?
- Do some of the books you currently read and draw from need to be shredded or updated?

By asking yourself these questions you are able to assess if the content of these books is pulling your perspective towards the south or north end of leadership. If you are drawing on books that keep your perspective narrow, you are leaning more towards the south-dwelling, external leader (remember status quo!). If you are reading books that expand your perspective, you are leaning more towards the north-sider, internal leader.

Step Two – Self-reflection (habits and assumptions)

Some books in your internal library are filled with the assumptions that *you hold*; others are filled with assumptions that *hold you*. This depends on who or what influences the content of the books. You may find it useful to reflect on the influences of the books using the questions below. You can also go back and reflect on your answers in the five-step staircase exercise in Chapter 4.

Questions

- Is the current content of the books in your internal library fulfilling and fuelling your purpose as a leader?
- Do you agree with the beliefs, values, traditions and memories that you are reading about?
- Are the beliefs, values, traditions and memories influenced by you or someone else?
- Do the beliefs, values, traditions and memories align with your internal *WHO* part and the leader you want to be?

By asking yourself these questions you can reflect on whose assumptions fill the pages of the books in your internal library.

Step three – Self-awareness (unconscious bias)

Imagine a gremlin sitting in a dark corner of your internal library. The gremlin rides your unconscious bias T-Rex to work every day. This gremlin not only writes all the content for your books but also tells you which books you are allowed to read. This gremlin wants you to stay in an endless loop of unawareness. The gremlin doesn't want you to know that you can take back control of what books you choose!

Your unconscious biases stem from the books in your internal library and the beliefs, values, traditions and memories they hold. Becoming aware of what kind of unconscious biases fill the pages in your books will strengthen your connection with your internal leader.

How can you become aware of where your gremlin is hiding and take back control? The questions below may help. You can also go back and reflect on the two self-awareness exercises in Chapter 5.

Questions
- What book is the gremlin handing you most frequently in your professional practice?
- Does this book align with your internal or external leader?
- Can you think of a book that aligns with your beliefs, values, traditions and memories as a leader?
- Is it time to fire your gremlin and shred some books in your internal library?

> By asking yourself these questions, **you** gain control of what unconscious biases are driving your leadership, not your gremlin. Maybe your T-Rex will get a little less hungry after this exercise!

YOUR FIRST AND ORIGINAL CHOICE – YOUR SEED

As I've mentioned, all the books kept in your internal library have been written, vetted and approved by you and your gremlin at some point in time. They all stem from your first and original choice, which I call 'the seed'. The seed is a core, internal choice that determines your behaviour on a very deep and unconscious level. Once you make this core choice, the gremlin grabs hold of this seed and gets to writing your books. Each time you confirm or reinforce this choice – this seed – the gremlin writes more frantically to ensure it is in *every* book it hands you. This seed penetrates your internal library, unconscious bias, habits and perspectives. As we know, these all have a profound effect on your professional practice and you as a leader. Recognising and understanding your seed is the key to self-regulation, personal mastery and unleashing your internal *WHO* leader.

Let's go back to Jasmin from the opening of this chapter to see how this can play out. Through our work together, Jasmin uncovered that her seed was 'I trust only myself'. This internal choice takes on an external form by her being busier than ever and spending more time at work than at home. This external choice has both positive and negative consequences. On the former, Jasmin is responsible and accountable for her actions and cannot place blame on her staff members. On the latter, this external choice of spending more time at work may simply be driven by her lack of trust. She needs to be present and in control, which is a by-product of only trusting herself. If this behaviour continues, the gremlin ensures that her seed is spread throughout all the books in her internal library. As a result, Jasmin will most likely become a control freak and micromanage her staff members, if she isn't already doing this!

Once the seed has been planted, every choice thereafter stems from this original choice. Jasmin's second choice was to start her own business. *How* she was going to operate her business had already been determined by her seed: 'I trust only myself'. Again, this choice has positive and negative consequences: she is able to be her own boss, but this comes with financial risk, government red tape and regulations.

Jasmin's third choice is another step out from the seed. After choosing to become a business owner (choice two), she committed to working hard *on* her business, not *in* her business. At this choice, her gremlin is working overtime to make sure the seed is pushed at every opportunity. By actively working *on* her business, she is rewarded with external achievements such as business growth and increased profits. On the flip side, this has led to a lack of quality family time or any time for herself.

As Jasmin's business grows, she makes her fourth choice to employ more staff. You can only imagine what her gremlin looks like right now, it's grown eight arms to keep up with book production. And you think you work hard! For Jasmin, a positive consequence of this choice is an increase in revenue and more team members to support further growth. A negative consequence of this same choice is Jasmin working overtime to ensure all tasks are performed to her standard rather than working *on* the business. The fourth choice that was supposed to support Jasmin and free up time at work has in fact *increased* her time in the business due to her seed: 'I only trust myself'. Paradoxically, the more staff that Jasmin employs to reduce her workload, the more her workload increases.

Very few people are self-aware of their seed; people tend to see only their external choices and not where they stem from.

The seed's ripple effect
As you can see from Jasmin's story, your seed has a ripple effect on all subsequent external choices. Imagine this seed as a pebble thrown into a still lake. Each ripple that emerges represents a choice that is made. Tracing back to your seed is the only way to make true change in your internal library.

1st choice – the seed	Positive consequence	Negative consequence
I trust only myself.	Only I am responsible and accountable for my actions.	Need to be in control, micromanaging tendency.
2nd choice – the first ripple	**Positive consequence**	**Negative consequence**
I will start my own business.	I am my own boss.	Financial risk, government red tape and regulations.
3rd choice – the second ripple	**Positive consequence**	**Negative consequence**
I am committed and work hard *on* my business.	Business is growing, profits are increasing.	Lack of quality time with family and myself.
4th choice – the third ripple	**Positive consequence**	**Negative consequence**
I employ more staff.	Increase in revenue, further growth.	Work overtime to ensure all tasks are completed to my standard.

By looking at Jasmin's story, do you think you can identify your seed? How does your seed impact your professional practice? Is your seed having intended and desirable effects on your leadership style? Is it planted in the north or south end of leadership?

In my story in Chapter 2, I unpacked how the traumas from my childhood set up my goal and dream to become a millionaire. I craved the safety and stability I was stripped of at a young age. It is clear that these emotions and trauma created my seed, handing over the reins to my gremlin. With each business opportunity I created, the seed penetrated every aspect of my life. It was only once I uncovered my seed that I could shred the books that no longer served me, fire my gremlin and plant a new seed in the north that reflected my healthier mindset and connection with my internal leader.

I invite you to go back and reflect on your answers from each activity in the chapters. By assessing your perspective, reflecting on your habits and being aware of your unconscious bias, you are beginning the journey of knowing where your current seed is planted. By knowing your seed and being an active choice architect in your life, you can dig it up and plant a new seed that better serves you as a north-side, internally motivated leader.

PART 3

In this final part of the book I will share with you some leadership transformations that will demonstrate how the leadership framework applies in practice. The following stories are based on transformations that I have had the privilege to be part of. The names have been changed to protect their privacy.

The leaders in these stories have all had a yearning to become an even deeper self-reflective, self-aware and self-assessing leader and active choice architect of their own life. They have all chosen to become gardeners of sorts, so they could propagate and nurture their seed.

CHAPTER 7
THE TRANSFORMATION JOURNEY

The initial impact of connecting with your north-side, internally motivated leader can often be hard to notice. When you change one part of your life, such as a particular habit, you may find yourself waiting for the ripple effect of your actions to affect other parts of your life. The wait for 'everything to fall into place' can be incredibly frustrating and disheartening and make you feel powerless. You may feel like you are stuck in an ocean rip, no matter how hard you swim towards the shore, you remain in the same spot or are swept even further out to sea.

In this time of transformation, many of my clients ask, 'Why should I put hours into transforming myself when I don't see any change straight away?'. My response lies with ocean safety 101:

Don't swim against a rip; swim parallel to the shore until you escape its grip.

Like with leadership transformation, taking the long swim around the rip and in to shore can be tiring, scary and overwhelming as you are surrounded by murky depths. Working through the uncomfortable facilitates growth, and as you toil through the dark water, you enable the connection between you and your internal leader to strengthen. As you reach the shore, you realise that you have successfully swum through your past perspectives, habits, unconscious biases and internal library contents, all that was holding you back from growth. Leadership transformation takes time, effort and courage, but much like the long and tiring swim to shore, it's worth it.

Think back to Vanessa Longgame and Peter Hare. Has either of them started their swim to shore? Do you think someone may still be stuck in the rip?

Now that you've reached the shore, let's see how your growth plays out in the workplace. Your leadership transformation has seen you change your perspective and rein in your biased T-Rex. However, all your immediate colleagues are pulled into the ocean you just escaped from, stuck in the rip of their closed perspectives and unconscious biases. You can't very well then start looking for evidence of your transformation in the external environment; for this, you probably have to leave this workplace or department and go elsewhere. Alternatively, you must be strong enough to withstand the rip and continue to connect with your internal leader onshore. In the long run, your newfound perspective may rub off on your colleagues and slowly change the organisational culture. Both options have pros and cons.

Another important aspect of internal transformation is to make small increment changes rather than one big paradigm-shifting change. A classic example of setting yourself up for failure is to make a big, sweeping new year's resolution, such as, 'I am going to stop smoking'. Of course, this is great in theory but most people fail within the first days or weeks of such a big change. Similarly, as a leader you may go away on a three-day retreat and feel totally uplifted and ready to change your leadership approach, only to fail miserably as you land back in reality.

So in addition to essential ocean safety 101, let's add a few more elements:

- Take small incremental steps towards change. This will ensure it is sustainable.

- Undertake frequent self-assessment, self-reflection and self-awareness activities (such as those in this book).

- Don't fear failure as it gives rise to new opportunities.

- Don't fear the uncomfortable; this is where change is most potent.

- Remember that your beliefs, values, traditions and memories shape your reality and determine your behaviour.

- Practise the art of pausing for a moment rather than letting your automatic system one thinking be in charge. 'Pausing' enables systems two thinking to take the rudder and steer you steadily to safe shores, away from T-Rexes and gremlins.

Each time you want to make a change as a leader, it requires you to dive back into that ocean, surrender to the rip and endure the swim to shore. External change is a ripple effect of your internal transformation and this arduous swim.

Internal transformation requires certain skills to be developed. The following framework links your required skills to the chapters in this book and their key takeaways, your internal library and your seed.

Required skill	Chapter	Key takeaway	How it links with your internal library
Self-assessment	Chapter 3 – Seeking a different perspective	South-dwelling external or north-sider internal	By assessing the **content** of the books in your *internal library*.
Self-reflection	Chapter 4 – Building habits that Serve	Assumptions that hold you or assumptions that you hold	By reflecting on **who or what** influences the **content** of the books in your *internal library*.

Self-awareness	Chapter 5 – Challenging unconscious bias	The connection with your internal leader vs. external leader	By connecting with your internal leader and becoming aware of *how* **your unconscious biases influence the content** of the books in your *internal library*.
Self-regulation and personal mastery	Chapter 6 – Transforming your internal library	Unleashing your internal *WHO* leader by uncovering your seed	By understanding that your beliefs, values, traditions and memories shape your reality and determine your behaviour. **You have the power to de-clutter** your *internal library*.

I'd like to share some real-life client stories and how I used the leadership framework to help them transform as leaders.

PROFESSIONAL ATHLETE ELANA

Elana used to be a professional athlete. She competed on an international level for many years. After her esteemed sporting career finished, she started her own successful business as a leadership coach and consultant.

Elana had been operating her business for more than a decade with many regular customers. Because of her athletic background and word-of-mouth recommendations about her unique approach, she was often inundated with more work than she could cope with (within a 40-hour working week). Once her children grew up, she often worked long hours and she was frequently away facilitating weekend retreats. Money was good and they lived in a beautiful house in an affluent neighbourhood.

When I started working with Elana, her business was flagging and she told me that she had lost her 'spark'. From what I could see, she was performing her role as a leadership coach with a task-based leadership perspective, rather than an approach motivated by the purpose that she displayed in the first few years of her business. She justified her task-based approach by claiming that her athletic career would be sufficient enough to maintain her business indefinitely. She also lacked the passion she once felt when engaging with her clients. Even though her business was suffering both financially and from a deteriorating reputation, she blamed outside factors.

She was also having difficulties with her physical wellbeing. As a professional athlete, she'd had to closely monitor her daily nutritional and carbohydrate intake. Her current mindset was that she now deserved to eat what and when she wanted to. Due to her extremely disciplined training regime as an athlete, she now found it hard to motivate herself to do regular exercise. Consequently, she put on some undesirable weight. Her relationship with her partner also suffered from a lack of meaningful connection (beyond the children) and an absence of libido.

Elana's story is not unique by any measure, I meet many people with very similar stories. Here is how I used my leadership framework to support Elana with her internal transformation.

Perspective

We started by assessing Elana's perspective by using the *'Assess your perspective'* exercise in this book. By the third deep breath, Elana trembled as she was breathing out. As I asked her Question 1: 'Why and how am I doing business at the moment?' she paused for a moment then started crying. With tears flowing down her cheeks, she let out all her fears and feelings of failure for letting her clients down and for not being present enough as a mother. My role here was to listen and validate her feelings. Elana had put an enormous amount of pressure on herself and had not given herself any space to breathe for a very long time. Our conversation, or more importantly the pausing for a moment, was enough to bring all her feelings and emotions to the surface. Her professional sporting career had taught her to block feelings of inadequacy, put on a brave face and get on with business. Elana realised through our many conversations that blocking emotions is detrimental to honest self-assessment.

Outcome – Elana realised she was too busy and lacked the time to be able to enjoy her role as a coach and role-model her north-side, internally motivated leader. Our conversations brought this into the light and enabled Elana to shift her perspective and once again role-model her internal leader.

Habits

At some point, we shifted conversations away from perspectives and towards habits instead. Elana shared with me that she wanted to get back into exercise but had tried and failed to build a sustainable exercise habit. She couldn't understand why she failed with this undertaking given she spent years training professionally. Elana told me that one of the reasons was that she was too busy to regularly exercise. The '*Ascending the five-step staircase*' exercise told a different story. In step three of the exercise 'Recognise assumptions that are getting in the way of your goal' it was clear that it was something much deeper than being 'too busy' that stopped her. Elana had spent many years training at an elite level and she was now held by her assumption that she had trained enough for a lifetime. Once her assumption was out in the open, Elana could reflect on the grip that this assumption had on her and we could work through it together. Her exercise regime started small with weekly incremental steps.

Outcome – Elana realised that she was held by her assumption that she had trained enough for a lifetime. By stepping through the 'Ascending the five-step staircase' exercise, she managed to build a new exercise habit.

Unconscious bias

The next phase of the leadership framework is to explore unconscious biases. With Elana now ready to tackle her task-based leadership perspective as a leadership coach, she was also ready to uncover her T-Rex. She had convinced herself that because she had been a professional athlete, she could leverage solely off her athletic reputation without the need to improve or update her approach. Of course, leveraging off her reputation worked really well at the beginning of her business venture when people still remembered her from her glory years. But now, years later, this was no longer the case. Interestingly, even though her business was suffering both financially and from a deteriorating reputation, she assigned blame to outside factors. During the exercise '*D.B.I.J. defence mechanism*', it was clear that she was in total denial about the long-term effects her task-based approach and lack of passion had on her business. The D.B.I.J. defence mechanism had such a stronghold in her that she could not see the truth staring at her: a decrease in revenue, fewer word-of-mouth referrals and less positive feedback from her clients. Yet, she assigned blame externally, rather than looking internally for things that were within her power to change. This, of course, meant that she was at the complete mercy of her starving T-Rex as it wreaked havoc on her mind. She was suffering from self-serving bias, the tendency to take credit for positive outcomes but blame external factors for negative outcomes.

Outcome – Elana's self-awareness increased by working through the 'D.B.I.J. defence mechanism' exercise with me. Consequently, she took responsibility for what was within her circle of control. She changed her approach, reigned in her T-Rex and took ownership of her deteriorating reputation and lack of new business.

Internal library
The most fascinating insights tend to reveal themselves during the transforming your internal library phase. At this point of the coaching, there is enough trust built up between me and the client that my questions can be formulated around beliefs and how they influence values.

Getting past the gremlin and uncovering the seed requires a lot of courage and willingness from the client as well as a lot of patience and gentleness from the coach.

When Elana and I did the *'Follow the money'* exercise, she initially shut down and we ended our conversation earlier than I anticipated. It was too much for her to take in, she needed time to process that her money was often spent on cafe catch ups with friends, enjoying coffee and sugary sweets. In the exercise, she attributed this to socialising and self-care. After years of strict eating as an athlete, Elana had developed the belief that 'If everybody else can eat what they want, why can't I do the same?'. She felt that she deserved to be able to eat what and when she wanted as a reward for years of dieting. She felt that she had nothing more to prove to the world anymore. Jackpot! We were now in seed territory! Together we uncovered that her seed was 'My worth is measured by my success in the external world'. Elana had spent decades of her life dedicated to being a professional athlete in a vain attempt to prove to the world that she was enough. Her exercise and eating habits were simply mechanisms of her seed, facilitating her quest to prove her worth through being a professional athlete. As her professional career ended, her consulting business grew from the same seed. Upon this realisation, the burden of her seed became unbearable as she came to understand the consequences it had on her business.

In terms of her eating habits, it was clear that her value about her body had shifted from 'my body is my temple' to 'my body is my amusement park'. Her strict eating habits as a professional athlete were, in her eyes, helping prove her worth to the external world. Elana realised that her current eating habits were also linked to her seed. As she consumed sugary sweets over coffee with friends, her gremlin continued to solidify the idea that her worth was linked to external factors like diet.

At this point, we shifted to the *'Three steps to declutter your internal library'* exercise. It is an exceptionally vulnerable place to be in when you open each book in your library and unfold your WHO layer by layer. We shared laughter, tears, anger, resentment, happiness, joy and fears that had accumulated from her past, present and future; all feelings and emotions were welcome and valid! We shredded the books and pages that no longer served her and fired her gremlin. Elana was now in control.

Outcome – Elana shredded books from her internal library that no longer served her. She unpacked the trauma that had caused her seed to take root deep within her.

Epilogue

Elana continues to flourish as a leader. Her strong connection with her internal leader enables her actions and behaviours to be motivated by her values rather than external factors. She has planted a new seed that she is nurturing and watering daily, with her gremlin nowhere to be seen. She realised that she was more than just 'an athlete'. Consequently, her business has shifted focus and now also includes stories from after her athletic career ended. Her exercise and eating habits are now serving her, rather than being an opportunity to prove her worth. Consequently, her personal wellbeing has improved dramatically. She has a much deeper connection with her partner and her libido is back again.

Elana has become an active choice architect of her own life and enriched her professional practice. She spent countless years dedicating her thoughts and power to that which did not serve her. By implementing the leadership framework, she has freed up time to continue to transform herself rather than holding herself back.

Here's how Elana's transformation fits with the leadership framework.

Chapter	Link to Elana's story	Exercise used	Outcome
Chapter 3 – Seeking a different perspective	She performed her role with a task-based leadership perspective, rather than an approach motivated by the purpose.	Assess your perspective.	Elana realised she was too busy to be able to enjoy her role as a coach. Our conversations enabled Elana to shift her perspective and once again role-model her internal leader.
Chapter 4 – Building habits that serve	She found it hard to motivate herself to do regular exercise.	Ascending the five-step staircase.	Elana realised that she was held by her assumption that she had trained enough for a lifetime. By completing the exercise, she managed to build a new exercise habit.
Chapter 5 – Challenging unconscious bias	She justified her task-based approach by claiming that her athletic career would be sufficient enough to maintain her business. She was stuck in the cycle of denial, blame, ignorance and justification.	D.B.I.J. defence mechanism.	She took responsibility for what was within her circle of control. She changed her approach, reined in her T-Rex and took ownership of her deteriorating reputation and lack of new business.

Chapter	Link to Elana's story	Exercise used	Outcome
Chapter 6 – Transforming your internal library	She uncovered her seed: 'My worth is measured by my success in the external world'. Elana had dedicated decades to her athletic career in a vain attempt to prove to the world that she was enough.	Follow the money and Three steps to declutter your internal library.	Elana shredded the books from her internal library that no longer served her and fired her gremlin. She unpacked the trauma that had caused her seed to take root deep within her and planted a new seed that better serves her.

BUSINESS OWNER MOHAMMED

Mohammed operates his own business. He truly enjoys the rush of ticking things off his to-do list and meeting with clients. Very little of his reflective time goes into researching new ways of growing his business or expanding his reach. Sure, when opportunities come his way, he jumps at them, but it is a haphazard approach. Mohammed sees himself as a doer, a true action man that gets things done. You may recognise Mohammed's approach in Peter Hare, from Chapter 3 – Seeking a Different Perspective, who loves working *in* his business rather than *on* it.

Mohammed shared with me that he wanted his products to have a wider reach. New sales were currently dependent on word-of-mouth and a website. My question to Mohammed was, 'How is anybody going to find their way to your website?' With a minimal marketing budget, advertising was not an option. From a business perspective, you can have the best product in the world but unless you have a supporting distribution network no one is going to know about your product. Customers can't purchase a product they don't know exists! A new business strategy was definitely needed.

However, the problem for Mohammed was much deeper rooted than simply producing a new business strategy. If a business strategy alone could solve the problem of sales, most business owners would have one. What was needed was an internal transformation so that a new perspective could form.

He, as a leader, had to change his internal perspective in order for the external world to look differently.

In one particular conversation, I gave Mohammed some homework, (which you may remember from Chapter 3):

- Define *your role,* not just the future employees' roles.

- Define how *your time* will be used, not just the employees' time.

- Define *your purpose* and how it is going to bring meaning and fulfilment, not just the employees' tasks.

This exercise is designed to trigger deeper thoughts about yourself within a business setting. It helps lift your gaze and look beyond the narrow goal of increasing sales. Mohammed and I took a few months to untangle his thoughts and ideas as his internal leader began to emerge.

Mohammed always believed that he knew all the answers and that his perspective was the 'right' one. He was unknowingly swallowing the blue pill by being wedded to the status quo mindset: all is good just the way it is, and if it isn't, it is not my fault. You can only imagine how challenging the *'Information self-assessment'* exercise was for him. Question 1.3 was particularly tough for him, *'Are you worried that you might find that you wasted years on doing something that did not align with your internal leader?'* The realisation that he had wasted valuable time weighed heavily on Mohammed and it took a lot of mentoring to support him during this difficult time.

During this exercise, Mohammed also shifted his black and white perspective, his 'you are either with me or against me' attitude. He realised that he had a chip on his shoulder and as a defence mechanism, he turned away most people who challenged him or didn't see things his way. This of course was very detrimental not only for those affected by this behaviour but more so for himself.

Outcome – During this process, his business vision and mission changed dramatically. More importantly, Mohammed was now connected with his internal leader and he practised the important art of accepting and rejecting the constant flow of information. He no longer saw challenging questions as a threat, but rather as an opportunity to grow. Mohammed is now an active choice architect of his own life with a deeply enriched professional practice.

Here's how Mohammed's transformation fits into the framework.

Chapter	Link to Mohammed's story	Exercise used	Outcome
Chapter 3 – Seeking a different perspective	Mohammed was wedded to the status quo and believed his perspective was always the 'right' one. He turned away people who challenged him or didn't agree with him.	Information self-assessment.	Mohammed realised that challenging questions presented an opportunity to grow rather than a threat.

CORPORATE LEADER FENG

Feng works in a corporate environment as a senior executive. He was tasked by the CEO to lead a huge infrastructure project that deeply affected hundreds of thousands of people. The media scrutiny was fierce and public opinion was divided into two main camps: for and against the project. Things were not going well for Feng when he engaged my services. Because of the pressure, he was suffering from a mental breakdown but continued to push ahead despite the warning signs. I had never worked with a client that suffered from the Dunning-Kruger Effect as much as Feng did. I discovered that the Peak of Mt Stupid was much higher than I thought it could be! Unfortunately that was not his only bias, he was also burdened by confirmation bias (amongst many others). He was literally swimming in cherry-picked data that supported his view and ignoring reputable data that contradicted his belief and that of his CEO. He was blindfolded and strapped to the back of his runaway T-Rex without a care in the world.

We began our work together with conversations and me shadowing Feng at work (i.e. silently observing him during his daily activities). He wanted me to observe his interactions and behaviours with colleagues and understand his work habits. He oozed confidence and charm but lacked compassion, perspective and understanding of personal space. It was always Feng's way or the highway; he had no listening abilities, no compromises and no empathy. From a corporate perspective, he was wedded to the status quo and his company was always right. I am convinced that had it not been for his deteriorating physical health, he would never have reached out to me for help.

For Feng, the real work started when I introduced him to the *'Internal feedback assessment'* exercise from Chapter 5 – Challenging Unconscious Bias. His trusted advisory boards were a mash-up of different versions of himself, all sucked out to sea in a big rip, sitting comfortably on floaties full of denial. With this lack of depth and breadth of his advisory boards, he could not recognise when something was a problem, even when it was in writing in front of him. He simply brushed the importance of it away with a comment, 'Who cares?' What followed was some pretty intense mentoring and debates about his wellbeing and how that may be linked to his biases and his lack of diversity in his trusted advisory boards. It was one long and extraordinary insight into the degrading power of Feng's D.B.I.J. defence mechanisms. The power of unconscious biases never ceases to amaze me. During our time together, Feng developed more and more self-awareness and eventually managed to see the world from a different perspective; it was a loooooooong fall down into the Valley of Despair before a slow ascend up the Slope of Enlightenment.

Outcome – Feng calls me his challenging lifesaver. He describes me as the most annoying but important person in his life as he climbed the slope of enlightenment. Interestingly, as Feng's self-awareness increased, he also shifted his CEO's mindset and the infrastructure project never got off the ground. Once Feng's awareness reached beyond his confirmation bias, he realised the immense environmental damage the project would have; this would have been a heavy burden on his conscience.

Here's how Feng's transformation fits into the framework.

Chapter	Link to Feng's story	Exercise used	Outcome
Chapter 5 – Challenging unconscious bias	Feng had surrounded himself with 'yes people' who were versions of himself and was blinded by numerous unconscious biases.	Internal feedback assessment.	Feng put in a lot of difficult work to understand his biases and turn around his attitude. He is now more self-aware.

WHERE TO FROM HERE?

When you picked up this book you were looking for a solution. You were drowning in doing, stuck in a rip. You may still be. But I hope I've convinced you that there is another way. A way that you can take back control of your life.

> **You and you alone are responsible for your situation. You and you alone have the power to change it.**

It's not an easy journey, but it's definitely possible. I know because I've been there and have guided my clients through their own journeys.

I've given you a whole lot of information and ideas, and I've asked you some confronting questions that you may not know, or want to know, the answer to yet. You might feel a bit overwhelmed and not sure where to start, and that's ok! There isn't one simple solution, one red pill you can take to make it all better; this is a life-changing process. The journey from south to north is a bit like a game of snakes and ladders: you will make progress some days, and lose ground others. But let me assure you, any work that you do on self-assessment, self-reflection and self-awareness is one stroke closer in your swim to shore. It's all part of the journey to be in a space where you can connect with your internal *WHO* leader and have personal mastery of your life. A place where you are no longer a slave to the system and are instead the active choice architect of your own life.

In the three case studies in Part 3, I used the full leadership framework with Elana, but just one element of it with Mohammed and Feng. Yet, as you saw, even working with one element of the framework helped Mohammed and Feng make the initial swim to shore. So be comforted by this and just make a start, every stroke counts. You don't have to do everything all at once.

I highly recommend engaging a leadership coach or mentor to share this otherwise lonely swim to shore. A coach or mentor will support you, remind you to be responsible for your actions and keep you accountable. Sure, this book gives you some exercises to get you started but it might not be enough. Connecting with your internal leader is a bit like the magic of childbirth: women can give birth to a child in complete isolation, however, most would rather have a midwife or doula who can coach them through this life-changing experience. Leadership transformation is similar in this sense. After being swept out to sea, having a coach or mentor to guide you back to shore makes the swim a little easier. Having a support network around you will improve your chances of success as you transition from an external to an internal leader. If you feel you need that extra support, I would love to be part of your journey as a mentor and coach. My contact details are at the end of this book should you choose to reach out.

EPILOGUE – THE EPIPHANY

I wrote this book from a space of lived experience!

When I was lost in external action- and achievement-based leadership, I didn't realise it. For a long time, I didn't recognise that my habits wasted my valuable time, my unconscious bias imprisoned me and that I followed outdated traditions like a sheep. My professional and personal life was about re-fuelling myself from the outside in. When cracks appeared in my facade, I first denied everything, then I blamed others, then I justified my actions and lastly, I ignored the truth that was staring me in the face (D.B.I.J. mechanism). It was too much for me to bear.

The epiphany eventually came through me: "To find the person who is responsible for where I am in life at this moment in time, I need to look no further than into a mirror."

This was the catapult insight that shifted my perspective and knocked me down from Mt Stupid. The leadership framework saved me from my destructive behaviours. It transformed my life, enriched my professional practice and improved my personal wellbeing.

You can also connect with your internal leader and create your own destiny. This book is here to support you as you pencil in the blank pages of your books with your stories and memories. By becoming an active choice architect of your own life, you are enabling your internal transformation to manifest in the external world.

Trust in yourself and create your leader from the inside out. Become the leader you always knew you could be.

THE END

CONNECT WITH ME

I hope this book gave you some insights. It would be great to connect with you and hear how it has helped you in your leadership journey.

If you need a leadership coach or mentor, or want to discuss how I can help you or your organisation to shift from the south to the north end of leadership, please get in touch.

I am also available as a motivational or keynote speaker at your next seminar, conference or event.

I look forward to speaking with you.

Website:	rivenconsulting.com.au
LinkedIn:	Robert Andersson
	www.linkedin.com/in/robertandersson1971
Email:	rivenconsult@gmail.com
Mobile:	+61 (0) 418 323 594
Twitter:	@Robert_A1971

Acknowledgements

This book is the culmination of my 30-year leadership journey – the ups and the downs, the successes and the devastations, the heartaches and the moments of joy and of course the lived experience from being a human being.

My biggest supporter is my wife, Vanessa. You have stood by my side for nearly three decades and have unconditionally loved me every single day. That says a lot about you, as most people that know me consider me to be uniquely intense and almost unbearably optimistic. But somehow you take my chaotic and never-ending energy in your stride. For me, you are the balance in an unbalanced world, the nurturing earth angel this space cadet needs to stay grounded. Goddess Vanessa, I love you beyond measure.

Our eldest daughter, Rayna, lights up the world with her calm and gentle approach to life. Rayna, you remind me of the importance of being true to myself. You are amazing!

Our youngest daughter, Nyah, thank you for being you. Your wonderful energy has no boundaries and I love being around you. You are extraordinary!

Our middle daughter, Finn, worked persistently with me on this book. She challenged every sentence and asked for clarification, leaving no page unturned. Finn, your ability to understand how I think and your support with filling in the blanks when I couldn't are unmatched. You have truly helped bring this book into the light. Because of you Finn, this book is clearer, more concise and more entertaining. You are incredible!

To Mum and Dad who taught me the three most valuable skills in life: the courage to love without limitations, the ability to forgive, and the wisdom to embrace the past and the negative while always looking forward and thinking optimistically. Imagine how leadership would look if every child could grow up under such circumstances. I love you Mum and Dad!

To my six siblings, thank you for helping me become who I am today.

To my dear friends in Australia and in Sweden, you have both challenged and supported me through all my endeavours; you know who you are, there are only a select few of you, so no need to mention names. I am truly blessed to have you in my life.

To my incredible editor, Lu Sexton, who somehow managed to get inside my head and understand the story and the message I wanted to share with the readers. Lu, without you being my 'task master' this book would have not been what it is today. Thank you for walking with me and keeping me on track.

To Kelly Irving, the book coach that every author needs – supportive, encouraging and as passionate as I am about my book. You have been with me from my first shitty manuscript to the final product and beyond. Your book structure templates and videos have really helped me get my thoughts organised. Your fortnightly Expert Author Group Coaching classes are tremendously helpful and the book focus friends you set me up with have made a world of difference.

My book focus friends, Adrian Jobson, Chris Sellers, Sarah Bass and Sharee Johnson have helped shape this book through conversations, debates, feedback and review after review after review. Our time together has been tremendously valuable for me as an author.

Colleagues from across the globe, you have all helped mould me into the leader I am today.

Clients who so courageously shed their masks and charades and replaced them with something uniquely personal. It has been an honour to play a small part as your inner leadership journeys has taken external form. It is a privilege and great honour to have worked with you.

Finally, I would like to extend a big thank you to you, the reader, for taking the time and having the trust to read the book. I hope that it gives you necessary skills to enrich your professional practice. May your swim to shore be filled with moments of clarity, and as you take that first step onto the sandy beach, remember how far you've progressed towards self-regulation and personal mastery.

CPSIA information can be obtained
at www.ICGtesting.com
Printed in the USA
LVHW022003120422
716028LV00006B/379